BLESSINGS
IN THE
SAND

BLESSINGS
IN THE SAND

THE ANTOINE NEHME LEGACY

Published by Advantage, Charleston, South Carolina.
Member of Advantage Media Group.

ADVANTAGE is a registered trademark and the Advantage colophon is a trademark of Advantage Media Group, Inc.

Printed in the United States of America.

ISBN: 978-1-59932-686-3
LCCN: 2016931661

This publication is designed to provide accurate and authoritative information in regard to the subject matter covered. It is sold with the understanding that neither the author nor the publisher are engaged in rendering legal, accounting, or other professional services. If legal advice or other expert assistance is required, the services of a competent professional person should be sought.

Advantage Media Group is proud to be a part of the Tree Neutral® program. Tree Neutral offsets the number of trees consumed in the production and printing of this book by taking proactive steps such as planting trees in direct proportion to the number of trees used to print books. To learn more about Tree Neutral, please visit **www.treeneutral.com**. To learn more about Advantage's commitment to being a responsible steward of the environment, please visit **www.advantagefamily.com/green**

To my father, my hero
Antoine Nehme

To my children and the children
of the entire family of Nehme
across generations and across the world

To the past, present, and future leaders
and staff of Nehmeh International Holdings

To all expatriate families in Qatar, the Gulf and worldwide

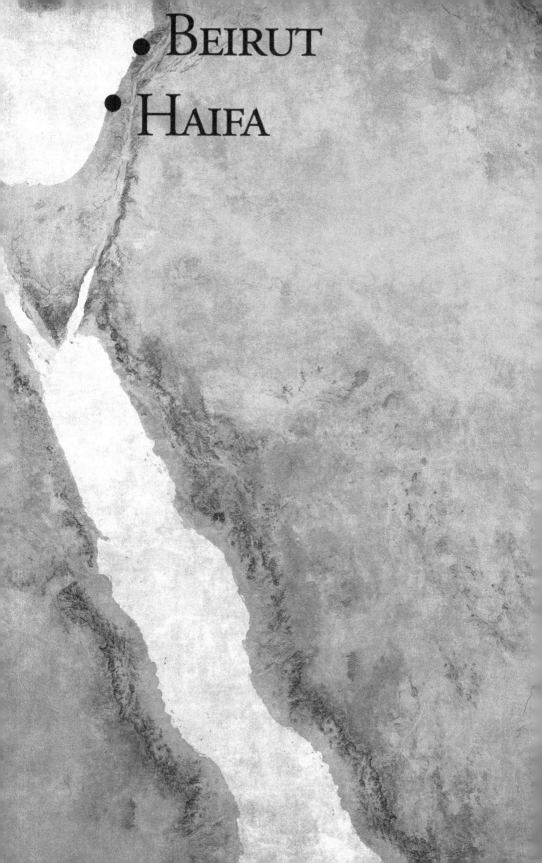

BEIRUT

HAIFA

BAHRAIN

DOHA

DUBAI

Table of Contents

Preface

I played around with the idea of writing a book for my departed, dear father in the form of a book of quotations, but it turned out there was a story to tell of a lifetime that just had to be recorded and documented.

There was also the issue of privacy, the respect for which we preach and practice. For this reason, this book was not supposed to see the light of day, especially the parts about my family! However, the messages and story of Antoine Nehme's life were so strong they broke through, producing a biography with various anecdotes and many thought-provoking quotations—and so this became my first book.

It serves the purpose of (a) documenting the life and times of Antoine to be shared with the Nehme families everywhere, (b) celebrating the sixtieth anniversary of the entrepreneurial birth of the business, and (c) supporting the charitable works of the Antoine Nehme Foundation with the proceeds from this book.

I often wondered what a worthy title would be for a biography that would take into consideration the depth and dimension of this great man and his legacy. It was easier than I thought, as *Blessings in the Sand* came naturally and evokes connotations of belief, good fortune, a journey, seizing an opportunity, and the ability to make things happen.

As you would expect, digging into the past in changing environments is a challenge. Due to the lack of readily available written records, some topics and dates have been culled from oral history.

The research methodology included looking for clues far and wide.

> *"Either write something worth reading,*
> *or do something worth writing."*
> —*Benjamin Franklin*

This book deals with important universal themes.

While it's a Middle Eastern real-life story about a Lebanese expatriate who came to Qatar for a new beginning, it is an immigrant success story, a very universal story.

Included are various stories of solid family values providing foundations for today's children as they flower into adults. A strong value is also placed on human resources in terms of how companies ought to be run and how they ought to treat their employees.

Antoine's life is a story that deserves to be told. Containing so much universal benefit, as it does, it is a success story worth sharing, worth reading, and worth discussing. I truly hope you learn from it and enjoy reading this tribute to a man who did so much for so many.

—*Alexander A. Nehme*

A Note from the Author

As Antoine Nehme's life was inextricably woven into the life of his company, trying to separate his life and his business would be like unwinding a beautiful tapestry to make smaller ones. This book is neither merely a biography, nor is it a business manual about how Nehmeh functions as a company. Rather, this book tries to maintain a fair balance between professional and emotional aspects of Antoine Nehme's legacy and convey the pride the Nehme family and Nehmeh International Holdings families have in that legacy.

The book's tone is meant to be neither pretentious nor doctrinal, as it must relate the history of both the company and a society. The use of explanatory language and quotations gets the meaning across more clearly.

Throughout this book, you will notice the words *Nehme* and *Nehmeh*. *Nehme* is the family name, while *Nehmeh* (with the additional *h*) is the business name.

Acknowledgments

My thanks goes to the countless number of people who assisted in the development of this book.

A special mention to Emil, Simon, and Rania for sharing all their memories and lessons learned from our founder and father.

I wish to especially recognize His Highness Sheikh Hamad Bin Khalifah Al Thani, the Father Emir of the State of Qatar, for his recognition and for having welcomed the very first Nehme in Qatar, where many members of the Nehme family still reside till this day.

Endless thanks to my beloved mother for her undying encouragement and belief in the value of this publication.

Naturally, no gratitude is complete without a special thanks to my wife, Joanna.

And finally, a sincere thank-you to the wonderful team at Advantage Media Group.

About the Author

 Alexander A. Nehme is the youngest son of Antoine Nehme and a partner at Nehmeh International Holdings, a multifaceted family business group serving the Middle East region. His chief officer responsibilities include corporate strategy implementation and group-shared services. Alexander A. Nehme is also a board member of various organizations and companies.

Introduction

At Nehmeh, we hold our heritage and our legacy in high esteem. While you may hear this from many other companies, we truly recognize the company's humble start through the efforts of one great man, Antoine Nehme.

With time, things are lost; things are forgotten. I wanted to find a way to avoid that, to especially preserve the legacy of a life so well lived.

At the same time, this book is not about merely reliving the past. We recognize and appreciate history and send this message continuously to our valued people who are part of an organization that has been around for perhaps longer than their own lifetimes.

> *"Each time you open a book and read it, a tree smiles*
> *knowing there is life after death."*
> —*Anonymous*

Nehmeh is even older than the country in which it was founded. As a family, we find this a very special trait in our company's history. Consider that Qatar, while having extremely ancient roots, gained its independence from the United Kingdom only in 1971. My father came to Qatar nearly twenty years before that, in the early 1950s.

Why is the company held in high esteem? The answer, quite simply, is because of the people who work for us. We believe they are our greatest asset and a main force behind the company's collective values.

Our company facilitates a lot of one-on-one engagement with our people, especially as we transition from six decades of operating as a family-run company to operating as a modern corporate structure with a board and relevant committees.

> *"The more you know of your history, the more liberated you are."*
> *—Maya Angelou*

While we are in the process of this transition, we consistently engage, individually, with the men and women who staff our company. It is a continual process that we know is appreciated. Many members of the staff have personally shared with me that their inspiration for working loyally for the company was inspired by Antoine, who passed away in 2010. This loyalty goes beyond our employees, however. When we travel around the territories we serve, we find people who still use the founder's first name, Antoine, when they speak of him. Many of our suppliers, our customers, and our staff fondly remember this man, who, from nothing, started what became Nehmeh International Holdings decades later.

All who remember working closely with this great man, more than five years after his passing, have very emotional recollections. I hope they find comfort in knowing that they belong to this great boat that Antoine once steered. It is a journey that started out in a very local and small way and now has regional and global aspirations, as we begin our seventh decade.

"A people without the knowledge of their past history, origin and culture is like a tree without roots."

—*Marcus Garvey*

The Nehme Family

The earliest records of the Nehme family can be traced back to AD 1517 in the Levant. The family's ancestral home was originally in the village of Lehfed in the Jbeil district of modern Lebanon, just a few miles from Byblos.

During the inter-religious civil war that plagued the Mount Lebanon area in 1860, more than sixty Christian families (including Nehme families) fled to the nearby town of Deir el Qamar in the Chouf district, while others went elsewhere, including—according to the oral traditions of our family—to the city of Haifa in what was then neighbouring Palestine.[1]

It must be recognized that within genealogy, family trees behave just as their natural cousins do, growing and intertwining time and again with other trees. Similarly, the Levantine family of Nehme (via the direct patrilineal line) stems from the Daou family tree, and both lines have comparable histories. In turn, the Daou family is believed to be part of the Ghassanids lineage, a group of South Arabian Christian tribes who emigrated in the early third century from Yemen and whose descendants were thought to be scattered in the Levant and in Cyprus.[2]

---

1   Source: http://www.adonisnehme.info/familytree/
2   Source: https://www.familytreedna.com/groups/daou/about/background

The Rags to Riches Story

Our company follows the classic Hollywood plot in its rags-to-riches story of the founder, Antoine Nehme. Ours is the story of one man who had nothing and who wanted to do something.

Antoine Nehme's history was even recognized by the leader of Qatar, His Highness Sheikh Hamad Bin Khalifah Al Thani. He had given our family a private audience with him at the Emiri Diwan, essentially Qatar's White House, so he could better know these Nehmes who had for so long been in his country. This was incredibly emotional for all of us, and the Emir gave us an hour of his precious time. There were ministers waiting for him to attend to important government business, but it did not matter. His Highness was having a good time reminiscing about the past with my father. During our visit, the Emir made us feel welcome and helped us recognize how important our family and Nehmeh were to the country.

I distinctly remember when His Highness told Antoine, "When you came to this country, I was a one-year-old." All in all, it was a huge affair and honour to have had that recognition as both a family and as a company.

The Nehmes are recognized as the oldest Christian family continuously residing in Qatar.

Antoine Nehme and HH Sheikh Hamad Bin Khalifah Al Thani,
Emir of the State of Qatar, in 2007

As a company, we are proud of this intense history of several decades. However, we also know we have a long future ahead of us. It is one in which we intend to keep alive the young and energetic spirit given to us by the founder. As a company in a rapidly changing world, we honour our past, but we do not want to be looked at as an obsolete structure with outdated processes. We have seen this to be the case for other large companies. At Nehmeh, we are heavily investing to streamline ourselves and to be continuously more modern in the way we work.

At the same time, we have not forgotten what a family is, either for ourselves as children of Antoine or for the men and women who work with Nehmeh and their respective families. I realize that when you invite any potential candidates to join a family firm, it does not go down as well as inviting them to work for a more traditional company. Additionally, there are companies that are family controlled but not necessarily family run.

A Company in Transition

"One measure of your success will be the degree to which you build up others who work with you. While building up others, you will build yourself."
—James E. Casey

At Nehmeh, change is one thing which we have embraced. While we children of the founder are highly involved in the day-to-day operations of the company, we are moving away from this model. We are working to empower delegations, teams, and committees to make the transition to a model in which the family has a less hands-on function.

Even as a traditional family company, we have always been ground-breaking. For instance, you might make assumptions about a company based in the Gulf, but when it comes to the over four hundred men and women working for us, it is very important to mention the women's role here. We pride ourselves that women are employed across the organization, from the bottom to the very top of the company. They include secretaries and other office staff, women supervisors and managers, and even a woman member on the board of directors.

This is something we feel is important to highlight. It is also something for which we know we are recognized in the region. Nehmeh is a comfortable place for women to work.

Our commitment to openness is evident: over twenty ethnicities from across the world are represented at Nehmeh. They come from countries in Africa, Asia, North America and Europe. It is something we pride ourselves on, and we are gratified to provide such a platform in Qatar.

While we love tradition and history, as a company entering into its seventh decade of operation, we believe that many old and outdated processes, systems, and procedures are no longer relevant. We know that our vision of being key players by 2020 requires a lot from everyone, both family and employees. We need to have people on board with the vision as we change.

The Importance of Family Values at Nehmeh

"Open your arms to change, but don't let go of your values."
—*Dalai Lama*

Family is key here at Nehmeh. When we say we get what a "family" is, you can be assured that family values are important to the company. We also know there is a modern definition of family, one that goes beyond our immediate relatives. Additionally, when we say "family," we also know we live in a day and age when *family* sometimes means nothing, unfortunately.

Family is an embodiment of values. When you lose that sense of unity, which is the real nucleus of a village or town or city or country or nation, you are on dangerous ground. We believe that applies to families, companies, countries, or any place people work together to achieve a common goal.

We understand this, as a company. It is something our founding father taught us long ago. We pride ourselves that we not only understand the value of the family name but also always work on a first-name basis to strengthen the ties between company leaders and the men and women working for them. It is a way to live up to our excellence and helps create an even playing field, a level, humble, low-key way of working together, rather than being in any way bureaucratic or overly formal. Our management has an open-door policy for our employees. Any of our employees can see anyone at any time with an appointment, and this is the atmosphere we foster at Nehmeh.

And how else do we emphasize our concern for our employees? Even though we are hard at work, we celebrate birthdays. With the current number of employees, virtually every day has a cause for celebration!

"One person with a belief is equal to a force of 99 who have only interests."
—*John Stuart Mill*

We are there in the difficult times for our staff. For example, as a company with family values, we assist people suffering grief in their own families.

We champion the successes of our employees. We also understand that the path to success can involve a failure along the way, and we try to give second chances. According to some outsiders, we may, perhaps, be too tolerant, but we know, as a family company, we cannot be any other way. Especially during the transition we are undergoing, it is important to be reasonably forgiving and allow people to adjust. We always tell staff they are allowed to make a mistake once but not repeat it. We even use the word *please*. We expect people to learn.

Nonetheless, we have our own code of business conduct, which we call The Nehmeh Way, and which involves zero tolerance for any behaviour conflicting with our ethics.

All of these strong values go back to the establishment of the family company by our patriarch, Antoine Nehme.

Opportunities and Fulfilling Client Needs

Antoine Nehme was the very definition of an entrepreneur. What is an entrepreneur after all? There is a challenge. There is a need. Somebody steps up to the plate to seize the opportunity and fill the need. This is what it comes down to. Antoine knew to answer opportunities when they came knocking. At the same time, I would not call him opportunistic, a word that may reflect negative meaning. Instead, I would call him someone capable of recognizing a right set of circumstances to fulfil a need through the complete sales cycle, not just sell and forget customers after they are through the door. At Nehmeh we take care of our clients and customers. Our business continues after the sale. We have service, training, customer relationship management (CRM), and customer service desks. We continue along on the journey with our customers, should they need our help.

Family Business

Let's take a look at statistics. More than 90 percent of the world's businesses are family managed or controlled, including some of the largest and best-known brands and companies. However, nearly all family businesses fail. According to statistics, 70 percent of family businesses do not survive into the second generation. Eighty-eight percent of family businesses do not survive into the third generation, and only 3 percent of businesses make it into the fourth generation and beyond, according to the USA-based Family Business Institute. I personally believe if a company does not have a combination of strong foundations, governance, goodwill, and some element of luck, then it is likely to fail.

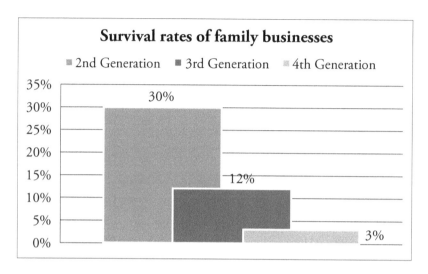

Source: US-based Family Business Institute.

Unfortunately, we have seen this all around us, from small families to the largest families. This might mean having to make constant compromises, sidelining decision making, and enacting incorrect strategic choices, thus weakening the company. Other family companies remain for far too long in control of the founding member, who might refuse to give up the reins due to lust for power or lack of trust, or the children might be afraid to take over, feeling incapable or not ready or simply unwilling. This inability to transfer power will, in most cases, destroy a company. For each family company to grow, there comes time when the torch must be passed to the next generation.

I am most proud of how my father transferred, in 1997, the entire business (and, literally, his name), with total determination, to my two brothers, Emil and Simon, who have earned it. I honestly cannot recall other examples of family businesses that have had the same seamless passing of the torch.

I am also proud to have witnessed the Arab world's only peaceful passing of power in recent memory, as in the case of H. H. Sheikh Hamad Bin Khalifah Al Thani, the Father Emir, who passed the leadership of the nation to his son H. H. Sheikh Tamim Bin Hamad Al Thani, Emir of the State of Qatar, in 2013.

> *"Remember, today is the tomorrow you worried about yesterday."*
> —*Dale Carnegie*

That is something we understand as a family company. It is important to ensure that business continues to be separate from personal life. People die, but companies should not. While we miss our founding patriarch, Antoine Nehme, we are happy that our company did not fail after his passing. He took steps, along with all his children, to create a process of continuity. What does the future hold for us in six more decades? We do not have a crystal ball. Nobody really knows what will happen in the future. However, we are making sure we will not fail in the future as we pass the company on to the generation that comes after ours. One way we are doing so is by ensuring our children gain experience with other companies and prove themselves in other arenas. For example, my own children, still currently in grade school, must prove themselves. If any of my own children want to work in our company, they must work elsewhere first. They must do well enough to get a promotion there as well. This validates their skills and qualifications so their subsequent employment in the family company is not merely nepotism. Once my children have crossed this line, a formal application can be submitted to the human resources department at Nehmeh—then and only then.

When we say we are a family company at Nehmeh, it does not mean that family name and kinship guarantees a job. Family members still need to be the best-qualified candidates. We have lasted sixty years, and much has happened in that time. There were wars in the Gulf and in the greater Middle East—some still raging as I write this—several economic crises, and increasing globalization of the economy. But we have survived and flourished while others have faltered and even completely disappeared.

Nehmeh Core Values

At Nehmeh we are always raising the bar. This is simply part of the DNA of Nehmeh and the Nehme family. We believe this is also why the company has not failed. In fact, we have thrived.

Our success has a lot to do with our values, once again.

At Nehmeh we have four core timeless values: people, quality, trust, and commitment. We put these values into the public domain in our literature and whenever we talk about our company to our stakeholders.

We believe that people are our most important assets. We recognize the company is about people. No people, no company. It is that simple. We know that the people who work for us need to be taken care of. They need to be sheltered, secured, enabled, and empowered.

We know that taking care of the needs of our people affects the next value: quality. As a family and as a company, we do not go for second best. We always want to be the best and sell the best. In other words, we want to set the standards.

> *"Quality means doing it right when no one is looking."*
> —*Henry Ford*

This concept goes hand in hand with our next value: trust. We have gained the trust of our people, and we continue to work nonstop to keep it, and this is not something we take for granted. Trust has no price and obviously cannot be bought at your local grocery store; you have to work consistently hard to earn it. People come to us to buy a particular product, service, or solution. We are there to offer it as it is. We do not hide anything. We do not lie. That is just not something we do.

This concept of trust starts with the personalities and characters of the individuals who comprise the board, the three sons and one daughter of the founder, Antoine Nehme. In order of age, we are Emil, Simon, Rania, and me, Alexander. Next year, we will add an independent board member. We are not scared of letting go. However, we are always vigilant that our core values remain anchors.

This, of course, explains the last value: commitment. Commitment is a promise. If I were to make you a promise, then you can bet I will keep that promise until the day I die. It is simply the way we do things. It is also a part of stating truths, as a family and as a company. Once we say we will do something, once we give our commitment, our promise, we follow through and we do it.

This is the Nehmeh DNA.

Brand Qatar

We are a part of Qatar, and Qatar is a part of us. If the Nehme family had never come to Qatar, Qatar would have still thrived, naturally. We were, maybe, a mere drop in the vast ocean of Qatar. Still, a few things come to mind when I say this. During the company's early days, our founding father always proudly represented Qatar, a duty which we continue till this very day.

Antoine Nehme (left) in Germany with a representative
of a local company (right), circa 1963.

He always had the Qatari flag with him. It was as if he were a Qatari official, if not, technically, a diplomat. Above is a picture that is very dear to me. Antoine (on the left) stands next to the old Qatari flag.[3] He is in Germany, proudly out and about, representing Qatar. The photo was taken in the early 1960s, before the country had gained independence.

---

3   This second version of the Qatari flag was first used in 1936 and highlighted
     the name of Qatar in Arabic along with nine diamonds representing the Trucial
     States (which later became the union of seven emirates under the United Arab
     Emirates), along with Bahrain and Qatar.

"As we express our gratitude, we must never forget that the highest appreciation is not to utter words, but to live by them."
—John F. Kennedy

The second way we have always represented Qatar is in manufacturing. For example, we were the first, and we remain the only, radiator factory in Qatar. All of our heat-transfer solutions (devices for cooling through oil, water, or air) are now made in Qatar. It was with great pride that we could add the phrase "Made in Qatar" to a product we built. We wanted to make sure our company was a part of everything pioneered in Qatar, to celebrate the country as our family's home base, and to promote our brand as one the world should know.

"Home is not where you are born;
home is where all your attempts to escape cease."
—Naguib Mahfouz

It is an important part of our philosophy. I am inspired by Gertrude Stein's words, which I have made relevant to the Nehme family: Lebanon is our country, but Doha, the capital of Qatar, is indeed our hometown. So the "Made in Qatar" label was very important, and it was, once again, recognized by the state. Around 1990, when we started this form of manufacturing, there was not much manufacturing in the whole of Qatar. Whatever was made in Qatar was extremely precious, a rare sight around the world. At that time, there were maybe fewer than a dozen companies using a "Made in Qatar" label. State officials would carry our brand and information about our factory whenever there was an exhibition anywhere in the world. Often, we were personally invited to accompany them.

Two and a half decades later, expansion of the oil and gas industries here in Qatar changed the manufacturing landscape. Many commodities are now fabricated locally, which is a great sign not just of Qatar's growth but also of its economic maturity. At the same time, with our sixty-year history, we feel that Nehmeh played a role, albeit small, in the success story of the Qatar brand. We are honoured to have been able to contribute to the transformation of Qatar into the wonderful modern country it is today, as recognized by the ruling family.

The company grew as Qatar grew; it was a hand-in-hand process. We also know, as a family and as a company, the country has come a long way from the early years of the last century.

The Origins of Qatar

Doha circa 1947

Qatar may not need an introduction in this day and age. However, it is important to understand the roots of this surprising country.

Prior to the production of oil, Qatar was one of the poorest countries. The great majority of the inhabitants lived at subsistence level with most of their income derived from pearl diving and fishing.

Due to the world economic crisis of the Great Depression of the 1930s, people in Qatar were starving and many died of famine. It is interesting to look back to that period and then to see, only twenty years later, my father coming to this great land. When he arrived, electricity was barely available. Only a few streets in Doha were paved. It was a typical third-world country, yet to stand on its own two feet. One could say Qatar was not yet a nation. It was waiting to be built by those born there and by those who would make it their new home, as Antoine did.

At the time, the population was tiny, estimated to be less than thirty thousand people living in the whole country in 1953.

Compare this with today where there are over two million people in Qatar at the time of this publication. From an economic standpoint, it was a very, very small market. Whoever was here either belonged to the local tribes that emigrated from the Saudi Peninsula or families that had been here even before that. A few families had come from Persia—Iran today—and some families came from India. All of this was, at the time, overseen by the British, who signed protective treaties in 1916. Today, when we reflect on the country's tremendous growth, it is good to see how proud the old locals are of this history. They witnessed so much over the ensuing decades.

A huge gamble was made on major investments in gas at the time. In some circles, skeptics were heard to say, "Gas is meaningless. It's hot air. It's a waste of time to invest in it." Time has proven that early investments in gas have paid off handsomely, making this country the world's largest exporter of LNG,[4] which resulted in Qatar's rank as the highest in GDP[5] per capita in the world. Investment in gas was a very wise decision! Qatar is now vastly wealthy, with a per capita income nearly three times that of the United States.

What we sometimes find, though, is Qatar's new generation may be out of touch because they were born to wealth. They never had to work as hard as those who came before them. It is not only the natives to whom I am referring. I am referring to all who are part of this society, which today includes large numbers of expatriates and other immigrant workers. The people who witnessed the transformation, however, tend to be more appreciative as they still recall how little they had and how much has changed. Of course, I do not mean to say that everybody else is unappreciative. Rather, people who undergo hardships tend to be more appreciative of improvements and, over time, proud of them.

This is not, of course, unique to Qatar and other parts of the Gulf region. We know that the children of immigrants everywhere in the world, from the United States to Australia and all points in between, find it hard to understand the struggles of their parents and grandparents. Here in Qatar, young people find it hard to imagine the struggles the country went through thirty years ago when they see air-conditioned shopping malls filled with all the world's goods.

---

4   Liquefied natural gas

5   Gross domestic product is national income/national output and national expenditure. GDP per capita divides the GDP by population size to produce the average income per person.

Of course, the shopping malls, highways, and skyscrapers are the glitter you see when you enter the country. I want to emphasize something much deeper in Qatar's transformation, something beyond the shopping malls. Qatar's infant mortality rate was among the highest in the world a few decades ago. Though invisible on the surface, the infant mortality rate represents another of the country's vast improvements as it modernized. Here in Qatar we have some of the world's greatest facilities for social welfare and health care. I have not even begun to tell you how much the local education system has improved over the decades as well, another achievement that is hard to see until you know the history of this great country and how it has improved in what is, in reality, a very short span of time. Oil and gas money were used to improve living conditions in a variety of ways for everyone who calls Qatar home.

Company Growth and Customer Care

Over the years, as Nehmeh's customers' needs expanded, we changed from importing to manufacturing. Powered by solid know-how, we developed the capacity to service the products customers bought from Nehmeh. This was also part of the simultaneous expansion of Qatar and Nehmeh.

The contrast of early Qatar with today's strongly consumer-based society in Qatar is remarkable. Back in 1953 there were few goods available, whether locally produced or imported and stocked. It was just a matter of time for the economy to move from importing items on special order to stocking items to have on hand at a moment's notice. Originally, our company imported goods and resold them. We would buy equipment from abroad and sell it at a premium. That premium was not only for profit. It was also to cover local warranty, service, repairs, parts, and often, payment terms as well.

As his business matures, a retailer will notice that some customers special-order certain items on a consistent basis. Rather than merely importing one such item at a time, the retailer begins to stock the high-demand items. It was in this way that Nehmeh moved from on-demand thinking—one unit once in a while—to keeping the item in stock, anticipating customers' needs. This was the series of transitions my father's company went through as it grew, along with the country and its economy.

There was even another logical step beyond this: servicing our clients and the products they bought from us. This concept of servicing meant establishing a fully fledged service and parts centre for anything we sold.

After the sale, we remain by their side. Customer care is part of our customer relationship management. Altogether, this is part of a company's progress to maturity, whereas, perhaps, in the past, you had one supplier of a particular product and you either took it or left it. The United States, early on, was like this—for example, with AT&T when it was a monopoly. When AT&T became too big, it was broken apart, creating competition. At Nehmeh we knew we had to be ahead of rivals and develop ways to give our customers more value.

When customer care included answering customer complaints, many companies stepped up to the plate. Companies had to start taking care of the tone they used with customers and how they reacted to questions and complaints. Whole policies needed to be put in place. People have to be trained to talk properly on the phone, to handle incoming equipment, and to honour warranties. For Nehmeh, there is also the imperative to ensure safety because we sell electrical and mechanical equipment, which if used incorrectly can cause injury or even death.

I always say this to my own children: "There are two kinds of people in this world: ones who rise above others through merit and others who exert all their efforts to bring down others above them."

This is how far we have come in this company built from nothing. It started with an idea one person had, a situation we have seen in other places too. It was not simply unique to Qatar. Still, we knew this was an emerging land, full of opportunities. Whoever was here back then could become significant. Whoever stayed to create a company, rather than being an employee, would also have a similar story to tell. There are many such families here in Qatar.

So when we talk about being built from very little, we know Antoine recognized an opportunity. He saw this country was still in its infancy when he arrived in 1953. He realized he could be part of its phenomenal growth. At the same time, he was a very humble man who also wanted everyone to simply know him by his first name, no matter how much his company grew.

Qatar had a small population in which everyone knew each other. "I bought it from Anton" was often echoed as many shops followed the name of the people behind the product, be they bakers, pharmacists, or grocers. What this tells us is that the people who sought out Antoine and the Nehmes were typical Qatar-based families. We had been in Qatar for so long we became part of the commercial fabric of the country. Whenever people had needs in any type of industrial work or construction, we were there for them.

This is, probably, what Antoine foresaw. He saw that his company could develop, rapidly or not. He wanted to be part of Qatar's growth because he felt he could add something. In this way, he could do well not just for his family but also for the market and for Qatar, his new homeland.

All this from a man who came in sandals to Qatar. This image will stay with me until the day I die: my father in sandals, landing in Doha's tiny airport. He came with sandals, the clothes on his back, and not much else. Sometimes, in his own recounting, he would say he arrived barefoot. Humility has always been an Antoine trademark.

He arrived from Beirut on a propeller plane. At the time, there were weekly planes connecting with Doha. Such planes often made stops in other parts of the Gulf—such as Bahrain, Kuwait, and Dubai—on their hopscotch journey. Doha had a sandy runway back then. There was no paved tarmac. Travellers would leave the plane after it landed on the edge of the town and just walk through the streets. That was it. There was no paperwork, no customs.

What a journey my father began in such a humble, simple way. He knew this also. In his own recounting to us, as children, he would also give a nod to what became my favourite Frank Sinatra song, "The Best Is Yet to Come."

We know that companies are about evolution, change, and constant redevelopment. Nations too are this way, along with the global economy. Companies can decide to stay the same, keeping the "old man" at the helm. In some circles, the mention of succession or the inevitable death of the same "old man" is considered taboo. Yet we know that is not in any way sustainable. The odds are you would leave and come back in a few years and that company would, probably, no longer be there. For Nehmeh, however, we like to think it has been a vastly different case.

Antoine Nehme, my father and the founder of Nehmeh, has passed on. Yet we can still continue his dream for his company and for this beloved country. Join me and my family as we embark on a journey on which Nehmeh and Qatar grew together.

PS: Although his real name appears to be Anton, as noted in some records, everyone called him Antoine. As for the family, the name Nehme is used (without the additional final "h"). Why, you ask? Read on, and you will find out why this is so.

CHAPTER 1

Sandals: Arriving in the Gulf with Nothing

"I cried when I had no shoes, but I stopped crying
when I saw a man without legs."

—*Unknown*

Antoine Nehme was born on January 15, 1930, in Haifa, Palestine, to a family that had emigrated from Lebanon. Named after Saint Anthony, Antoine's birthday is traditionally celebrated on January 18.

One has to think about the society into which he was born. This was a period in which there was no such thing as television or many of the other things we now take for granted.

As the eldest of eight children, Antoine felt responsible for all his brothers and sisters—four boys and four girls in total. His father had served as a railway inspector on the Haifa–Beirut–Tripoli train service and later entered the textile trade. He was old and could not always be relied on to be the family breadwinner. As identified in the Introduction, Antoine's family was originally Lebanese but, by the late nineteenth century, had settled in the port city of Haifa.

It was in this city that Antoine was born and raised. As an adolescent, he was first introduced to the world of commerce there, as it was a very large business hub at the time. Haifa was the place to be in the Eastern Mediterranean. It was a fairly young city that had grown mainly because it lies on the coast, and it was here that the British created their ports for oil flowing via pipelines from Iraq and Saudi Arabia. Trade and competition between Beirut and Haifa was particularly intense, both by land and sea. There was a lot of interaction with foreigners, whether those in the vicinity of the German colony, a historic district within the city today, or the many other Europeans living in the region. At the time of my father's birth, Haifa and its surroundings to the west and south were part of the British Mandate, controlled by the British Empire after World War I and the breakup of the Ottoman Empire. What is modern Lebanon fell to French control at the time. Thus, the region was full of Europeans, those who visited the ancient sites and those who looked to do business here, other than the official and military presence of course.

At the time, the links between Haifa and Beirut were well established by road, rail, air, and sea, which allowed ease of movement between the two cities. This exposure to people from various backgrounds explains why Antoine Nehme's business never differentiated based on race, colour, or religion.

My father had gone to school through the secondary level, what the Americans call high school. However, he did not have enough money to go to college. Still, as this was part of the British Mandate, English was among the languages that he learned. Arabic was his mother tongue, and he also knew French. His studies were also conducted at the Collège des Frères school (the Catholic order of the Brothers of the Christian Schools).

As a smart young man, he started by being an accountant at the Iraq Petroleum Company (IPC) in Haifa and later learned electrical maintenance of engines and vehicles (he loved to work with his hands) in the Saifi district of Beirut, Lebanon, for better opportunities.

"Our greatest glory is not in never falling, but in rising every time we fall."
—Confucius

At the end of World War II, this area underwent rapid, violent transition, which culminated in 1948 with what those of us of Arab descent call the *Nakbah* (catastrophe) when many families were expelled from their lands. Many, such as my father's family, went back to their ancestral home of Lebanon, arriving with nothing more than what they could carry. My father and his family chose Lebanon because it was close and their family roots were there. They took shelter in one of the local Christian monasteries dotting the region.

> *"We can throw stones, complain about them, stumble on them, climb over them, or build with them."*
> —*William Arthur Ward*

By this time my father had reached the age of eighteen. He was an able young man, but some of his siblings were as young as three or four years of age. Still, each of them had to do something to assist the family.

In the immediate aftermath of this forceful expulsion, the family lived in Lebanon as refugees, essentially in absolute poverty. Life consisted of scratching out a living as best as they could. I remember listening to the hardships distinctly from family stories.

My father often mentioned that Christian Arabs recited this mantra: "May God always repel poverty from you," reminding him of the tormented hungry nights experienced early in his life. Many nights, they were unable to sleep because of the trauma and shock of the events that had unfolded. Today, we understand the plight of wartime refugees a little better, as television and the Internet show us what they are experiencing.

> *"Change is the law of life, and those who look only to the past or present are certain to miss the future."*
> —*John F. Kennedy*

The tragedy also meant a certain practicality in terms of work: the family would do whatever it could to earn whatever was possible. One thing my father always said was, "No matter the work, no work is shameful." It was important to think this way early on to ensure the family's survival.

While he was a very young man, an opportunity arose for him, in 1953, to go to Qatar to work for a company by the name of Contracting and Trading Company (CAT), which itself was originally established in 1937 in Haifa. Before 1953, as you can imagine, my father would do anything for the sake of work. This ranged from heavy lifting to performing labour of any kind—whatever it took in times of desperation. In recounting these stories, my father told me that until he was asked to work there, he had never heard of Qatar. Rather, he had heard of Bahrain because that country was an important hub for the Gulf region. It too was controlled by the British, as Haifa once was.

A Propeller Plane

Airplane travel at the time was still something rare and unusual, especially to emigrate to faraway places such as Europe and North America. The families of those who were leaving would not only wave goodbye to them but would also act in such a way that it was almost a process of mourning. Family members would wear black as if they were at a funeral, in the belief that it would be the last time they would see or hear from their loved ones. You must remember that in the middle of the last century, communication was very limited. Air travel over great distances was also difficult or even prohibitive due to its expense. It is not the same today when you can message from a cell phone or book cheap air travel on the Internet to flying back and forth easily across the world.

After leaving Beirut, my father landed in Doha, not knowing what to expect. He only had heard bits and pieces about what the country was like. I know little of these first years. While my father had not told us all the details, I imagine he stayed here with many roommates because he did not have his own place.

For two years, Antoine worked with CAT here in Qatar. What exactly was he working on? That is another good question. The answer remains a fuzzy haze to his own family. My father always told us he was good with his hands. His mechanical skills could be considered advanced relative to conditions at that time. He could fix anything you brought to him. This included all things mechanical—engines, vehicles and even electrical items as well.

Technology in 1950s Qatar

While we can only catch a glimpse, in our minds, of what he was working on, we know that my father's contract with CAT was for two years in Qatar. After those two years had come to pass, the company told him, "You're done. You can go home or you can stay." And my father decided to stay. He decided this for the many reasons we discussed earlier. He saw there was opportunity for him. At the same time, there was a strong need for his skills and his knowledge. He had been exposed to the trade industry while in Qatar, and he recognized there was a need for some sort of a hardware store in the country.

In 1955 he decided to establish his own hardware store. Evidently, he did not have his own store right away. He still needed to get his things in order, and some of the details of his life then remain obscure to us. We do know, however, that he spoke of the scarcity of various commodities during this time. Electricity and modern appliances would solve this, but the country, at the time, had only limited electrical resources. As there was no electricity, staying cool in 40 degrees Celsius—over 100 degrees Fahrenheit—of desert heat was no easy task. This applied to both cooling humans and food.

In the Gulf countries, many structures used to be built with what are called wind towers. These are not the towers you think of for wind-power generation but open, box-like structures on the roofs, with slats promoting airflow. You see them in classic images of old Gulf architecture, and even some modern buildings pay homage to them in their design, though the wind tower in such cases is purely decorative, not functional.

A typical wind tower of the Gulf.

These wind towers are based on a concept that is simple and ingenious: because warm air rises, whatever is left below becomes a bit cooler. In addition, whatever small breeze may come through the vertical windows at the top of wind tower creates a whirlwind, similar to that of a ceiling fan, exhausting the hot air to the outside and keeping the cooler air in the lower spaces. Later, our founding father recalled, he had to manually spin fan blades to circulate air.[6]

6   Great resources on Qatar back in the day:
https://originsofdoha.wordpress.com/history-of-doha/
doha-1916-1971-from-a-british-protectorate-to-independence/
http://catnaps.org/islamic/islaqatold.html

Even in the 1950s, when American families were up late watching TV in well-lit living rooms, people in Qatar, where electricity was scarce, went to bed by sunset. With the advent of improved electric utilities, that changed. At one time, the country relied on oil lamps and candles for lighting past sunset. The whole country was off the grid, as we would say now. Delightfully, stories back then were told to scare children from playing in the dark because parents did not want them to get lost. Spooky stories kept kids at home so they would not go out into the unknown.

"I will walk by myself and cure myself in the sunshine and the wind."
—*Charles Reznikoff*

We have photographs of these old buildings in our family collection, along with images of my father in front of such buildings, sandals on his feet. It was in this environment that my father began to think more deeply about modern technology. While these ancient cooling systems work well for traditional structures of small size, they do not work for large modern buildings. My father knew that as Qatar modernized, it would need more electricity and people to service these modern conveniences.

This was how virgin the environment was where my father settled in the early 1950s. Contrast that with Europe, rebuilding after World War II, or Italy's Dolce Vita period, or the United States with its automobiles and all those interstate highways emerging across the country. Qatar had only two paved roads at the time. Even the ruling Emir preferred tents rather than the opulent structures of modernity. My father would tell us stories of how he would casually wave to the Emir, H.H. Sheikh Ali Bin Abdullah Al Thani then, who would be in his tent with two guards at his sides and strike up a conversation with, "As-Salaam-Alaikum, How do you do?" It must be noted that Qatar has always been a closely knit tribal society, yet Antoine Nehme was able to gain the respect of members of many local prominent families, including the Al Thani, the Al Mana, the Al Rumaihi, the Mannai, and the Darwish, among many others.

A Qatari trait that I appreciate is what might be described as the local version of a gentlemen's agreement, but in reality, it is interpreted here beyond someone just giving his "word"; it is a real oath carried to the grave. Perhaps it is a product of the harsh environment or the simple structure of local society from a bygone era, but this trait remains alive and well. Should a man give you his "word," you could rest assured it would remain so until that person's death. However, should you betray this trust, you would be put out as an outcast, along with your children and even your children's children.

The situation was very humble for locals and for those who came from other countries, who were still few in number. In some ways, I might compare it to the Wild West of the United States, still being built, with its sense of promise. At the time, it also was not a place where you would see large numbers of foreigners, as you might now. Nomadic Arabian tribes were naturally all part of the community for generations, along with a large number of immigrants from the Indian subcontinent. This was because of trade routes established long before modernity and based on fishing, ancient trade, and pearl diving, the original forms of the local economy. The British, though small in number, controlled the territory, reporting back to London. There were, however, very few Lebanese immigrants like my father who decided to stay and to hold on.

Daring

"It isn't the mountain ahead that wears you out;
it's the grain of sand in your shoe."
—Anonymous

For me, my father is one of the bravest men I have known, but I also believe that in this new environment, he must have had his fears. I am sure he questioned his purpose in being so far away from his family. He would not see them for many years until the late 1950s and early 1960s when he began to bring them over, welcoming his brothers, his mother, and his father to this new land he now called home.

Antoine Nehme, circa 1950s.

Yet we know he persisted and grew stronger in the new environment in spite of his apprehensions, including homesickness and, perhaps, difficulty with the local Arabic dialect that was so different from his own Lebanese way of speaking the language. Arabic differs from English in that the written word is somewhat different from the colloquial one. Even more different is the actual pronunciation of various words. One example is the spelling and pronunciation of Antoine Nehme, which was localized to Anton Nehmeh, the source of the additional *h* in the Nehmeh company, emphasizing the *eh* ending. And, quite simply, he was an alien in a new place, a new country, one he knew so little of. Imagine going to a place where you might not see your family for quite some time, alone with limited communication channels. At the same time—and this is a very important point for us in our family history— whatever money he made, he would send home to Lebanon because his family depended on it for their own survival.

"Success is how high you bounce when you hit bottom."
—*George S. Patton*

Thinking about this and other stories he told from that time period still gives me goosebumps. He recounted to us how he would spend his nights on the edge of starvation, going to bed hungry to maximize his savings in order to send all the money back to his family still living in Lebanon.

That is how poor they were back in Lebanon and how much he sacrificed for them. That is when I think the idea was cemented in his brain to declare war on poverty. He did not want anybody to experience poverty as he had. He felt a huge sense of responsibility to do the best he could for both his family and for the society that provided him with so many opportunities.

"Hardships often prepare ordinary people for an extraordinary destiny."
—C. S. Lewis

My father's own deprivation made him ever more determined to strive, not only for himself and his family but for other people. It is for these reasons that my father remains a hero for myself, our family, and for the men and women working at Nehmeh.

CHAPTER 2

Spark: The Drive and Determination
to Be One's Own Boss

"A pessimist sees the difficulty in every opportunity. An optimist sees the opportunity in every difficulty."

—Winston Churchill

The Transition from 1953 to 1955

There is a spark, a *cri de coeur*, when one says, "I can't have this anymore. I must do something about it." It is a time when things have to change.

For my father, Antoine, that cri de coeur was his arrival at the decision to leave Beirut, having had enough of the poverty he was encountering there. As a young man, he certainly had a desire for adventure too, wanting to challenge himself with the unknown and the adventure of it all.

As a family and as a company, we have to look back now, sixty years later, and ask ourselves what this initial spark was and how bad things were in Beirut at that time to make him want to go to Qatar. Why leave Lebanon and the love of family to head to a place that had what seemed like nothing?

Looking back, we believe there was a push and a pull: the intense deprivation and poverty that pushed him out and the sense of adventure that pulled him to Qatar. It was not enough for him to observe poverty; he was motivated to end that poverty by heading off to another place. Now, we live in a time of websites such as Kiva.org, arab.org, and other socially conscious Internet platforms. We can work where we can affect change, better ourselves, and ask the world for help. Back then, this was a complete unknown; people did things for themselves, out of their own necessity. Poverty was always there. It was certainly not unique to Antoine.

We can say that, once again, he had a leap of faith in 1955 because his decision to stay meant being alone. He would no longer be guaranteed a job or a place of shelter. This must have resulted in tremendous anxiety, not least of all because whatever money he would make, he would send directly home.

"If opportunity doesn't knock, build a door."
—*Milton Berle*

We have to ask ourselves, looking back more than six decades, why Antoine didn't return to Beirut. We might think it's a very good question, but to my knowledge, there were more opportunities to be found in Qatar than in Lebanon. Lebanon was more established back then. It had infrastructure and was somewhat peaceful. Antoine's decision to remain in Doha took all these factors into account. A pioneer, he would take a risk. He would try to do something. He felt he would be successful. My father was an extremely persistent kind of person. He was continually knocking on the door of opportunity. He was a relentless man in that respect, and that is why we wish to honour him and all he was able to achieve in Qatar.

"Do not go where the path may lead;
go instead where there is no path and leave a trail."
—*Ralph Waldo Emerson*

By 1955, all of this played into why he decided he no longer wanted to be an employee. He wanted to be his own boss so he could hold his destiny in his own hands rather than continue at the mercy of others.

It is this idea that is the spark, the moment when things change, for Antoine, and thus, ultimately, for all of us who are descended from him. We know he was continuously challenging himself. While he was always good at what he did for his former employer, he knew he would be replaced if he failed. If he succeeded, he would share this with his friends and family.

Awake to Opportunity

Should you lose the location of your seed	ان فقدت مكان بذورك
Which you have once implanted,	التي بذرتها يوما ما
Rain will whisper to you its location.	سيخبرك المطر اين زرعتها
So plant goodness over any land	لذا ابذر الخير فوق اي ارض
And under any sky, and with everyone.	و تحت اي سماء، و مع اي أحد
For you do not know where or when you may find it again.	فأنت لا تعلم اين تجده، و متى تجده؟
Cultivate a deed even it is not in the right place	ازرع جميلًا ولو غير موضعه
As goodness can never be lost where it is planted.	فلا يضيع جميل اينما زرعا

We know from stories my father told us about this time in the middle of the 1950s that after arriving in Qatar, even when he was tired, he would not sleep. He would sometimes say he was always awake. In later years, I understood his meaning: he harnessed his energy and remained awake to opportunity. I am certain the serenity of the desert night sky allowed him to think clearly.

Antoine worked continuously. He also studied consistently. He didn't study books in the traditional sense but, rather, whatever catalogues and manuals he could get his hands on. In his early days after leaving CAT, when he was on his own, he might fix a car, or learn a new industrial painting process, or perhaps it might be electrical work. He was always trying, always extending his knowledge.

This was the spark and the adventure. It was the change that developed in his viewpoint between his arrival in Qatar in 1953 and the end of that first assignment in 1955 when he made the decision to not be an employee anymore and to become his own boss.

Yet, as large as our family of four children feels to us, his family was much larger. It also fell to him to be the breadwinner during a time when Lebanon was in constant flux. The Lebanese economy was sluggish. It was not a land of opportunity, even if it was a place of immediate shelter.

It was for these reasons that, ultimately, he decided to leave Lebanon.

Qatar was a small country that very few had even heard of, but it offered plenty of opportunities, as he would come to know. There was almost no electricity in Qatar. My father foresaw something that we and others perhaps did not recognize.

"All men who have achieved great things have been great dreamers."
—*Orison Swett Marden*

With such a new place, anything was possible. He saw real opportunity for progress on this land, allowing him to start anew, perhaps to build a dream for himself and his family. There was generosity in the land of Qatar, and because of this, my father was able to open a store of his very own after a brief time. The country was growing, and so were its demands.

Qatar was in need of many products and services. There was a saying at the time that "if you need anything, go to Anton." Antoine's store was like a supermarket for electrical and mechanical needs. He began to see how much business and how many opportunities could be seized and created. It is important to highlight that the relationships he established with European and Japanese partners (among many others) during the late 1960s and early 1970s remain to this very day.

"I deserve better."

—*Antoine Nehme*

I believe his responsibility at CAT was not challenging enough for him. He thought he deserved more, not necessarily in terms of pay but in terms of responsibility. He had more skills than the ones he used for particular tasks with the company that had brought him to Doha. He wanted more, as an individual, and to feed his family.

My father also had a philosophy that we know drove him at this time: "Never be an employee. Be your own boss." He repeated this phrase to us, and we know it was in his mind when he established his own company.

He did not want to be at the mercy of someone else. Looking back, we can say it might have been for one of three reasons: he might have had a bad boss, he might have been a bad subordinate, or he was just an innovating ambitious person. He was always improvising and trying to find new ways of doing things. Knowing my father, I would say that he had ideas of his own and was always a collaborative kind of fellow, but perhaps his boss rejected his ideas or would not listen to him. As his children, we knew him to be this way: someone always trying to involve others in his plans.

Antoine Nehme treated people exceptionally well whenever he met or worked with them. Unfortunately, he might not have always received this same treatment from others, especially those who were above him in his first job in Qatar. I think of his behaviour as a case of reverse psychology: he treated people the opposite of how he, at times, was treated. All of this might have factored in his wanting to become the employer and not remain the employee.

Quite ironically, the original company that brought my father here is one of the companies contracted with the task of rebuilding the entire heart of the old city, which included the demolition of Antoine Nehme's original store.

Overcoming Obstacles to Move from Surviving to Thriving

When my brothers and sister and I look back at this time, what we also realize is how many obstacles our father was able to overcome in his life. He had many struggles from a very young age that many of us would find hard to imagine. They ranged from surviving the *Nakbah* to overcoming intense poverty, to bringing his family with him to Qatar. Antoine was able to strive, not only for himself through all of this but also for his family. He had an intense passion to be able to make it through obstacles and to determine ways around them. He was beaten down at almost every turn by circumstances in the Middle East, yet he figured out ways to make more of himself.

Antoine Nehme, circa 1960s.

One reason might be that he was always a very religious man. He would pray continuously, in good times and bad. Among his prayers was a request for God to look after his immediate and extended family. I tend to believe one reason for this was the heavy toll that being the breadwinner exerted on him, especially as his father was not in the greatest health.

After 1948, my grandfather was no longer working, no longer able to be productive, which meant that his children had to work. They did anything they could to make a living for the family. One of the children, for instance, became a tailor for a time. Others worked, temporarily, in transport, others in a pharmacy and in any form of labour possible. Still, the family needed more money to survive.

It was these exact circumstances that led Antoine to Qatar. Once he was there, he sent all his money back to his family. He also ate in the company canteen to save as much money as possible. This all paid off, allowing him to completely turn his financial situation around. In 1956 he began bringing his brothers as well as his mother and father to Qatar. Afterward, he started travelling back and forth to Lebanon and other parts of the region. By 1963 he had purchased land in Lebanon to construct an apartment building that included accommodation for members of his family along with apartments he could rent for additional income. Qatar remained his home base throughout this time.

My father's role had moved from helping the family to survive in Lebanon to a situation in which they began to thrive.

Still, through it all, Antoine remained a humble man. He worked very long hours early in his career in Qatar, and his main form of transportation was a bicycle. A bicycle? It might seem crazy, looking back, as who cycles in Qatar today, in the heat? But back then it was a necessary form of transport. There was no mass transit and virtually no vehicles of any kind. At one point however, his bicycle was stolen. When this happened, he may have thought it was a sign that he should leave his office, his work, and go home. Yet he persisted.

Today we might label Antoine a workaholic, but he also knew not to get himself worked up when things went wrong. The right thing would eventually happen. My father had a tremendous amount of resourcefulness, which shows in his dedication to making a living and doing anything he could to ensure it.

"Persistent people begin their success where others end in failure."
—*Edward Eggleston*

At the beginning of his time in Qatar, his money transfers were all about survival. Eventually, with the apartment complex in Lebanon as evidence, things would get much better. Antoine was doing well; he was doing more than merely helping his family. Eventually, when motor vehicles started becoming more available in Qatar, he purchased two of them, a tremendous luxury at the time.

In just under a decade, he had gone from employee to employer and successful entrepreneur.

Yet this all happened after overcoming tremendous obstacles, the kind most people never overcome. They pushed him to succeed, especially with so many younger siblings looking to him as a beacon of responsibility and leadership. Imagine having an entire family looking up to you for guidance!

Still, we ask what it was that made Antoine Nehme strive. At times we can only guess; we can only make an assumption that still leaves a question mark lingering at the end. Was it having seven brothers and sisters? Was it the hard knocks when he was young? What was it that made him strive?

"Self-trust is the first secret of success."
—*Ralph Waldo Emerson*

As we reminisce about those early days, we can conclude how Antoine figured out how to work his way out of poverty. When we look at stories of other successful men and women, we know there can be a variety of reasons for becoming what they did. There is the notion that being an immigrant makes someone want to strive even more, no matter where he or she settles, be it Qatar, Australia, France, Canada, or the United States. At the heart of it, this is the immigrant struggle: Antoine wanted to prove his value to his family back home in Lebanon and especially to his new home in Qatar, which gave him so much opportunity. Most of all, perhaps, he wanted to prove it to himself I think. Whatever the reason may be, he has left a legacy of inspiration for all of us related to him, and all of us who are part of the Nehmeh family at work in Qatar and elsewhere.

CHAPTER 3

Start: Building Castles in the Sand

"To achieve greatness, start where you are, use what you have, do what you can."

—Arthur Ashe

A leap of faith naturally involves risk. Antoine had to play his part to be pioneering. On one hand, he saw a need and an opportunity that needed to be fulfilled. On the other hand, he had to implement all of his know-how to feed that need. When I look back at his difficulties and while I know he ultimately succeeded in life, I am sure there were many times when he experienced failure. These setbacks, of course, were not necessarily part of the narrative he told his children. My belief, though, is that he learned from his many attempts and failures and built on his successes in order to become the man we remember.

Antoine saw the need for hardware, automotive solutions, and automotive parts and launched his company.

His first idea in building what became a successful business was to provide products to the local market in Qatar as that country developed. I am sure there were fewer than a dozen cars back then, probably owned by the British colonialists and Qatar's ruling family. Whatever they required, he would have been there to supply it, as a handyman. His knowledge and skills became more important as buildings went up. These might not yet have been the glittering skyscrapers we associate with the Gulf today, but they were new buildings, nonetheless. They were only a few stories high—small, certainly, but we all start somewhere, as people and as countries.

Antoine Nehme, circa 1950s.

Antoine's first shop had a single door and no window. The building still stands to this day, though, at the time of writing, it is slated for demolition for a large project. This storefront was in the heart of Doha, which, in the more than sixty years since his arrival in this great city and country, has grown exponentially. The photo we often use in our company literature is of another one of my father's stores that opened across the street after he shifted from the initial storefront.

Anton Nehmeh store circa 1960s.

At the time he moved into the region, the currency was Indian rupees, as there was no local currency produced by the government of Qatar then.

Various accounts from this time also resonate with me as I consider our founding father's life. To the very end of his days, Antoine was always passionate about machines and equipment. He always told me the greatest thing for him was to visit factories. He loved to understand how things worked, especially how assembly lines flowed from raw materials to end product.

One thing that comes to mind and is based on the same principle is how he loved to watch orchestras play. He would see how the conductor led the band in a synchronous performance. In some ways, I think he saw himself belonging there—where he could see what needed to be done and take charge of it. He truly felt he could make a difference. Whether fixing a car battery or simply doing a touch up on something, he was always able to lead and do so in a humble manner.

The store he created was a warehouse for spare parts. He was one of the first to import vehicle tires into Qatar, stocking a renowned European brand. All of this became significant to the growth of the country.

My father would also bring in goods and test the market as it grew. Sometimes he was successful and other times he was not. Yet through it all, he was fearless in trying something new in this new country, the literal definition of a pioneer.

Anton Nehmeh circa 1960s.

Pursuing the Blessing

Antoine was a very young man when he began to achieve success. He was just twenty-three when he arrived in Qatar, and by the age of twenty-five, he was out on his own to make a living and a name for himself. With all due respect, today you will find most twenty-five-year-old men lost, completely unable to figure out life. Here you have a young man of twenty-three years wanting to build a better future for all: for himself, his family, and his new country.

It is important to realize that Antoine's main concern was bringing his mother and father to Qatar. He had already overcome obstacles, but as early as the age of twenty, he wanted more for himself and for those he loved. It is relevant that my grandparents' household was one of the first to have television, made possible by the hard work of their son Antoine.

As an *independent* businessman, Antoine pursued the goal of taking his family away from their difficult situation in Lebanon. One phrase he often used is "Pursue the blessing." In other words, we must follow the blessing wherever we find it. Qatar, he had found, was a land with many blessings. It was a country that was good to him, one that responded by favouring his hard work.

Through his hard work and the support of his circles, he was able to later start a store that carried his name. It was simply called Anton Nehmeh.

How much of a groundbreaker was my father and his store? The post-office address explains it all. His Doha post office box number was a double digit. In other words, he and his company were among the first one hundred in Doha to even have a post office box for mail delivery. To this day, mail for the company is still received at this same two-digit-numbered post-office box.

Shop decal highlighting post office box 99, circa 1980s.

How many companies do you know of that can list themselves not only as among the first hundred to have an address in the capital of a country but also to still be around today, more than six decades later?

It is also essential to understand that though my father built this incredible company and legacy, he was very hands-off with us when it came to the transition period. He wanted to know the big picture, not just the bottom line. He was painting in grand strokes for us, making us think about the future and how to lay out plans for it. He asked such questions as, "What's next? Where are we going as a company? What are you doing to get us there? What are the steps for expansion?"—things along these lines so that we thought beyond day-to-day profits and toward sustainability and how we would eventually transfer the company to our own children, his grandchildren.

These ideas of legacy and longevity are important points. The company is the family, and the family is the company. And as a family, we actually put our heads on the line and believe so much in what we do. This dedication in family companies leads to tremendous success not only within the company but also the community—a fact backed by the Family Business Australia (FBA) board in the statement, "Research has shown that consumers believe family companies make products they can trust and are more committed to their communities more so than their public counterparts." We are constantly working to continue earning such a belief.

The move to changing the company name to solely "Nehmeh" was made in 2009, and all our companies were rebranded this way. We put our name and reputation on the line every day because of the values our founding father taught us and how he started the company: by being patient, correct, and honest with people. This is how we operate with each other as a family, as siblings, with our employees, and most of all, with our customers, whose trust we have merited to deliver their needs.

It is for these reasons that though Antoine passed away in 2010, the company he founded (along with its core values) strives in the hands of the second generation preparing for the third.

CHAPTER 4

Growth: Nehmeh's Growth
Alongside Qatar's Spectacular Rise

"Never say you are tired. Remain energetic always."

—*Antoine Nehme*

"I always tried to turn every disaster into an opportunity."
—John D. Rockefeller

The company grew exponentially in its early days. We can say much of it was due to Antoine's skills, especially his understanding of how to go after opportunities and pursue unfulfilled niches. Yet we also know at the heart of it was an important symbiosis: my father's company grew as the nation of Qatar grew, modernizing over the decades and spurring exponential population growth.

Of course, it is not that the company caused Qatar to grow; it was a combination of circumstances and the synergy between everything that was going on. Quite simply, Qatar gave the company the opportunity to grow.

Antoine Nehme at his shop circa 1970s.

The Nehmeh's growth also mirrored phases the nation went through: we went from importing to manufacturing to growing our service industry. Qatar, as a nation, grew in this same way. Early on, this great nation relied mostly on importing products, along with the know-how of people who grew up in other places, as my father had. The concept of "Made in Qatar" was also something that developed in concurrence with our own patterns of growth. We cannot necessarily say we created the label that is now known around the world. Still, by the 1990s, when we began to place this label on our heat exchangers, we were among only a handful of companies manufacturing in the country.

> *"Business has all five senses, just like a human being."*
> —*Antoine Nehme*

To radiators and other heat-exchange devices we added many other lines of products and services, including more offerings to the automotive, construction, and woodworking sectors. We also expanded service solutions for the aftermarkets. At first this was done to help our customers with products they purchased through us. We also help our clients plan their own company's expansions through consulting services in such areas as improved flow techniques. I believe this kind of business service was something Antoine envisioned decades ago when he toured factories almost for fun, fascinated by the way assembly lines and other manufacturing processes were formulated.

*Antoine Nehme alongside the largest heat exchanger produced
and proudly "Made in Qatar" circa 1990s.*

As Doha turned into a thriving metropolis, he strove to meet the ever-increasing demands of the country. With the oil boom, more people relocated to Qatar seeking work opportunities in this desert nation. More people meant more housing. They required more cars. Whatever was a necessity, he somewhere and somehow wanted to be part of that. He recognized and became a part of every opportunity that made sense for his family company.

Tradition and Growth

We must also look at those early years around the 1950s when everyone worked together to build a new society with new ways of doing things even while retaining traditions.

Because Qatar was, quite frankly, a virgin territory back then, Antoine saw many opportunities for him to play his part in contributing to a country that was in rapid development. He was among the first to import tires along with aftermarket vehicle batteries. In addition to supplying equipment for the repair of motor vehicles, he also serviced vehicles, from electrical to other kinds of repairs and maintenance. His company also stocked machinery other companies would need, along with the spare parts. Keeping things on hand for his customers in Qatar allowed him to work faster and more efficiently. When something was urgently needed, he no longer had to wait the tremendous amount of time it took to order a new part from the United States or Europe.

> *"It requires a great deal of boldness and a great deal of caution*
> *to make a great fortune, and when you have it,*
> *it requires ten times as much skill to keep it."*
> —*Ralph Waldo Emerson*

Whatever the country demanded, "Anton" was there to fulfil it. For almost any product a company could wish for, he would answer with it right away. If any customer complained, he would immediately fix the problem. When people were not satisfied with something, he went out of his way to make sure they became satisfied.

Was that a typical way of doing business in Qatar? Or was it because everything was new—new for everyone, for customers, and for my father?

Building a Modern State and Society Together

The community that was native Qatari was very small in number. While my father found a way to live and thrive here early on, Qatar was not very attractive to foreigners. The discovery of oil and its subsequent revenue changed things. Labourers and professionals had to be brought from outside the country. They ranged from construction workers to teachers, nurses, doctors, and experts in many other fields. This also meant the new society had to be tolerant of new ideas, new technologies, and new machinery processes because all of that was needed to develop the infrastructure.

In Qatar this meant going well beyond what is under the ground. It meant having an accessible network of maintenance bays for pipe fittings, wiring, utility equipment, and so on. There were also the day-to-day matters, such as building new schools with the required and correct infrastructures and amenities. Such new schools were being built every day. As the country modernized, motor vehicles came to function more and more in the lives of Qatar's population, requiring more paved roads to be created.

All of that became part of the transition of a traditional backwater state to a modern one. It required grasping new concepts, for the indigenous peoples especially. And even though many of the old ways were out, naturally religion and some of the traditional customs remained.

It was in the massive transition from a very traditional society to an industrial one that Antoine's store filled an important role. It was not a restaurant or a place of entertainment or other luxury. Rather, the store was about providing necessities to a country in the process of development. Unsurprisingly, as Qatar grew and more people came in, competition started popping up. Antoine was no longer the only one to recognize opportunities in front of him, which meant he had to work harder to maintain the important role he had developed over the years.

In Lebanon

We have already discussed how my father acquired land in Lebanon to construct an apartment building to house his family and to provide rental income. Beyond real estate, Antoine Nehme also founded the

Nehmeh Radiator Factory in 1974 (the first factory of its type in Lebanon), which he would later hand over entirely to his brothers.

In the UAE

Although it was short-lived, it is important to recall that Antoine Nehme had set up a trading outpost in Dubai prior to 1965. Administrative reasons were to blame for its closure. We are just now reclaiming a footing in the Emirates after more than fifty years of absence.

In Bahrain

In very early communities, you see copyists—people who duplicate. One baker might open shop right next door to another baker. To stay ahead of the competition, many of whom were copyists, Antoine had to improve his systems and work flow. From importing to manufacturing, he added new lines of products and services.

We have also had to implement new systems to handle growth, which included expansion into the neighbouring country of Bahrain in late 2010, after my father's death. At the bottom of it all, though, was the fact that his company's basis in Qatar was the reason for its huge synergy and growth as that country developed.

Once we were established in Qatar, there was a natural desire to expand into other parts of the region, and Bahrain was a natural growth area for Nehmeh. Bahrain is a friendly country very close to Qatar but not without potential risks. Highest among them was opening our business under a new set of rules. Since it was not possible to treat that particular operation as a branch of the main company, we had to change our systems. We had to approach Bahrain on its own terms.

A sense of empowerment was required; power would be taken from one place and put somewhere else. Transferring power creates friction, which is stressful because you start thinking, "Wait a minute. Who used to call the shots back then? Who oversees the new branch?" We took that problem to heart.

Despite challenging times—and challenges continue to arise with new situations—we always follow our vision. The Nehmeh vision is what allowed us to become a regional key player. It keeps us on our toes. Bahrain was an important milestone because it marked the first time we reached out to international territory. We wanted to replicate what we were doing in Qatar and see if it could be successful elsewhere.

We could not allow it to fail. We could not allow business in Bahrain to close down because that would have had an impact on our morale and the self-esteem of our entire organization. We said Bahrain would be the first point of expansion. After Bahrain, we have goals of expanding into other territories. We know there will be a second and a third and a fourth country we expand into. That is our drive and our vision. The store, the concept, or even the activity itself may change, but our presence will surely remain.

> *"You must have long-term goals to keep you from being frustrated by short-term failures."*
> —*Charles C. Noble*

This potential expansion reminds us that we need to highlight how Qatar has been very good to my family. The country not only welcomed us but allowed us to live and operate a business in it. This great nation gave us a platform and a stable foundation from which we could expand. Branching out was a natural process. It was not that the Qatari market became too small. It was that with such success there, we saw a need for our products, our services, and our presence in other markets.

Antoine Nehme in Europe, circa 1970s.

When we did the initial business plan and scanned the markets, we asked ourselves if there was a need for Nehmeh in a foreign territory. Indeed there was. And when we launched our new business in Bahrain, the whole management team was invited there. It was truly an exciting event. Even five years in, the special feeling continues to resonate. The launch occurred in 2010, but we had been planning it since 2007.

I would say in the past eight years, while other companies were just putting out catalogues left, right, and centre, asking potential clients to thoughtlessly buy, buy, buy, with a lack of concern for their needs, we made a conscious decision to invest in ourselves. We decided we had to concentrate on our core. What makes us different? What makes us special? What are the reasons why customers come to us? How can we uphold that?

Bahrain was an important mountain to climb, and we had to climb at a careful and deliberate pace. Every now and then a challenging situation arises in Bahrain, be it economic or political or operational. And when this happens, we do scratch our heads, but we also tap our chin and remember our expansion and its own learning curve. We want to make sure that whatever we get into, we do so for well-considered reasons. We are therefore methodical in planning and execution, and this shows not just in how long we have lasted but also in how long we have thrived.

After all, our more than four hundred employees translate into more than four hundred families who depend on Nehmeh. As we are aware, some people have more dependents than others. Using a factor of three, we estimate that over 1,200 individuals depend on Nehmeh. We know these people are reliant on this company's success and growth. We always remember this huge responsibility.

The interesting thing is that my father passed away in the same year we expanded into Bahrain. He passed in July 2010, and by the end of that December, we had opened our Bahrain office. We had been toying with the idea for some time, and we had involved our father in our discussions and process.

We asked ourselves if it was the right time to expand. It was, after all, just a few months after Antoine had passed away. We were saddened, yet we were resilient. We said to ourselves, "We have a company that serves as a capsule of wisdom—it has witnessed dozens of crises, and so the journey must continue." We knew the best way to honour him was to continue to thrive rather than endlessly grieve. Had we turned our focus inward, we would have forgotten whatever plans we had in place for a company. Once we opened in Bahrain, we certainly wished Antoine was among us, as it was a very important milestone in our history.

The Bahrain opening ceremony had a formal and official launch, with the whole management team travelling from Qatar to Bahrain. We invited everyone, from Bahraini ministers to local businesspeople.
Not to sound overly sentimental, I believe that he was there too. In fact, my father is still here. What was clear was that as we continued his journey, we were keeping his legacy alive and well. No matter the crisis, be it death, wars, or other events out of our control, we will still be around. As a company and as a family, we become stronger and develop greater unity in challenging times to keep the momentum going.

"We do not heal the past by dwelling there;
we heal the past by living fully in the present."
—*Marianne Williamson*

Among my father's sayings was that our company has feelings. If you are sad, the company will be sad. If you are asleep, the company will be asleep also. We must, as company leaders, shape up and rise to whatever the circumstances are.

Press Release

> Nehmeh's commitment to providing clients in the region with the best-quality products and the highest level of customer service will once again witness a major boost with the upcoming launch of its newest showroom that is situated in heart of Bahrain. Nehmeh is excited to unveil this latest

addition to its rapidly expanding family of first-class retail showrooms and equally confident of the positive impact of this investment in our bottom line as well as to the strength of the Nehmeh name in the brotherly country of Bahrain.

— Emil A. Nehme, 2010

2010 was indeed a special year. After several decades of operations, we felt it was time to grow. We would love to have had our founder in Bahrain with us, but even without him, we were following his message to keep going.

Through all of the challenges, my father's voice was always with us. Even in times of rest. When I try to relax, I still hear him saying to me, "Get up. Go be productive. You should go do something beneficial, be it to your pocket or to your health. Just do something. You can't just stay still. You can't stay idle."

"Good health and peace of mind are of essence."
—Antoine Nehme

What we have found with the company is that growth is something positive as long as it is sustainable. You cannot simply be a one-hit wonder and disappear. In order for it to be sustainable, you need to plan, and in order to plan, you will need to have all the right tools and all the right information. As long as companies, people, and families plan and plan correctly, the odds are they will be more likely to succeed than to fail. And, importantly enough, it was all right to change plans to adapt to the dynamic environments.

Similarly, Qatar, once it began to develop, was never idle. The country's growth was phenomenal. It expanded into every industry, into every requirement of a modern state. Visitors to Qatar know very well that with each return visit to the country, something new will have taken shape. Such is the way of rapidly developing countries—they promise a surprise with each visit: new infrastructure, streets, buildings, and even new cities!

Qatar came from so little. I still remember when camels roamed not too far away from our house. One favourite story I recall from my own childhood is about driving to an industrial area of the city to open a branch. We had to slow down to let camels pass before we could continue our journey. Looking back on that experience, through Western eyes, I think it was like a scene from *Lawrence of Arabia*. There was desert all around us, too—a harsh desert—and no matter how much you tried to tame it with air conditioning or other vanities of modern man, Mother Nature was still stronger.

I recall that you could leave a house unattended for a while, only to find desert shrubs and sand all around it when you returned. That part of sustainability—maintenance, staying on top of the impact of Mother Nature—is always difficult and always a challenge. For me, I liken this to our company and the environment it faces; despite what is and will always be thrown our way, we must continue to maintain and survive. We must keep doing what we are doing: expanding, modifying, main-taining, keeping the momentum, and ensuring we do our part for our social and environmental targets. We will come back to the topic of sustainability later in this book.

CHAPTER 5

Family: The More Personal Stories

"If you're blessed, then be generous for God will keep an eye on your loved ones."

—*Antoine Nehme*

As a family company, family is the most important thing to Nehmeh. We are a very traditional Lebanese family, yet we are also progressive. It was in 1990 that we also became a company where the transition from the founder to the children was also beginning, and my older brothers began to take on many more of the company's functions. We are a family with a strong physical resemblance to each other and a profound love and respect for each other and for my father and the values he instilled in all of us.

In this chapter, we will take a close look at all of us and how we became both the family and the family company we are now known as.

A bit of chronology is necessary, of course. In the early 1960s, the family purchased land in Lebanon for a residential building. After that, from his humble beginnings, Antoine remained the breadwinner for the family. One by one, he brought his brothers to Qatar starting with Alfred (known locally as Fareed), then Abdallah and Youssef. This helped to increase income and stability for the family, with everyone living and working together under one roof.

Brothers of Antoine Nehme.
From left to right: Abdallah, Alfred, and Youssef, circa 1960s.

It was my grandmother's request, just before 1965, that Antoine not get married, because she wanted him to continue on his journey to being productive and successful. She wanted him to finish completing the land acquisition and the construction of the apartment building in Lebanon before marriage.

Once that occurred, my grandparents took note of a beautiful woman while they were visiting friends and relatives. They told my future mother they knew of someone who would make a good husband for her: Antoine, of course. Naturally, back then, Lebanon was the most conservative of societies, even though the country was more open than many other countries in the region in the 1960s.

My parents' marriage was not arranged in the way we think arranged marriages are organized. Rather, it was arranged by way of introductions and with my father knowing he was expected to wed. The story was that his family was told there was a woman whose friends and family thought would be a good match for their son. They told Antoine, "Why don't you come by? There's this woman we'd like you to meet." The message was clear.

She Said

The story my mother told me about this major event in her life, indeed in all of our lives, was of this big, tall, handsome fellow coming in to meet with her family driving a brand-new vehicle (apparently a Mercury Comet). As the families knew each other, she was also aware that this was some form of arrangement. The important thing was that she and my father met, and the attraction was mutual. By December 1965 they were married.

My mother travelled for the first time to Qatar in early 1966. This new country was alien to her due to its desert landscape and its being less developed than, and far from, Lebanon. Beyond that, supplies were also difficult to get for a growing family. She remembers that on every Tuesday, fresh meat would be flown in by plane from Lebanon and elsewhere. Though she could not remember the exact day, fresh vegetables were flown in from Cyprus and Lebanon, too.

In due time, my older brother, Emil, was born, followed by my second brother, Simon and later my sister, Rania, and then myself. Parenting was a most important role. As Antoine was the bread earner, my mother had to look after the studies for us children. We had no tutor, as might be common nowadays. My mother was also the housekeeper of her own home.

The newlyweds, circa 1960s.

She was on her own in the sense that her Lebanese family was not there to help. She worked very hard. Additionally, my father's brothers, mother, and father were also in Qatar. This created a busy place for my mother, away from the support of her own parents and siblings.

I am comfortable in calling my mother old fashioned because I do not mean it in the negative way many people may think of it today. My mother was the source of many of the values that brought us to where we are today. I believe one can be old fashioned and modern all at the same time. As an example, we can converse with each other through instant messaging, but even this represents good old-fashioned values. People want to communicate in person, even over thousands of miles, and technology enables this. So many challenges had to be overcome for us just to be able to talk on the phone using the most modern technology in a peaceful setting. The concept of being old fashioned when it comes to values is something I hold dear and I appreciate in my mother very much.

She was a traditional Middle Eastern mother. She was not involved in work because with four children and the rest of my father's family coming to Qatar early on, somebody had to take care of the house. If my father managed the office with his staff, then my mother managed the home with the family.

Father made his influence felt in social and professional ethics; Mother established the moral grounds at home. Lucky are the children whose parents complement one another because this results in children with high moral values.

"Water is the softest thing, yet it can penetrate mountains and earth. This shows clearly the principle of softness overcoming hardness."

—Lao Tzu

When I describe my mother as a typical Middle Eastern mother, I say it with complete pride. It is indeed a luxury today for a mother to not have to work outside of the home and to be able to spend most of her time with the children. Dedicated mothers are not mere housewives, but they actively build the character of their children, identifying where their strengths lie.

I believe this is extremely important. When you work the whole day and come back home to spend maybe half an hour with your children, you miss out on so much. That is why time with one's children is a real treasure. Time is truly more important and more precious than gold. Looking back on this, I believe the values that were embedded in all of us as children would not have been possible unless my mother had been a career woman—that career being motherhood. She did it—I can honestly tell you—wonderfully.

This was part of being a team with my father: staying at home and raising the children. There was a professional side and a personal side.

Each one complemented the other. While Antoine worked in his profession, my mother made sure we recognized right from wrong. She gave us our moral values, our own customs and traditions—all together. All of these were hardwired into us along with the constant and comforting sense that we, as children, were special and valued and not strangers my parents had "found on the street." That builds character, confidence, and self-esteem. When we see how some families fall apart, the importance of taking care of the children becomes more apparent.

Though their functions were at opposite ends of the professional-personal spectrum, my parents had values in common. As children, and now, as adults, we would never lie. We were open. We were honest. Of course, as do all parents, my parents faced problems of one sort or another, but they were aligned in the sense that they really wanted to raise their children to be exemplary adults with a genuine sense of integrity. Everyone could see what my parents had done, and I believe this shows in the strengths we now have in running the company as a family.

As a family, we enjoyed a great amount of respect, education, exposure to other cultures, and travel together. We were given the opportunity to learn a number of languages, including Arabic, French, and English, among others. All of that came as a true blessing when we moved beyond Qatar for studies, as young adults finding our places in the world and back at home. We also never forgot that this is where the family name came in. The name Nehme literally means "blessing." We appreciate this, and we do not take anything for granted. Our philosophy is to value everything we have. At the end of the day, we all leave this world with nothing. In our tradition, when it is all finally over, we will each be granted a three-day funeral service attended by family members and friends wearing black and drinking Arabic coffee. I believe you should cherish every moment you are alive and try to make a positive difference in the lives of others.

The essence of life is a strong family bond. Family is that secret club you were born into, that you love, and with which you are familiar. Family is a place to let your hair down and be whoever you want to be. It is a place where you will not be judged. Certainly, there will be an argument and a fight here and there because as children's minds develop, egos grow. And it's not just egos that grow but also stubbornness and perhaps determination too, which has a value of its own and is something I admire because you are going with an idea no matter the consequences. Our arguments made our family bonds even stronger, something I appreciate all the more as an adult. Such values, especially that of determination, instilled in us as children and young adults were important as we prepared for the company's transition in 1990 and are still important as we continue to grow the business.

Health was highly regarded by Antoine Nehme. He always advised us to leave the dining table hungry and never to overeat. His words can be translated to mean appreciating what you have, taking only what you need, and never overdoing any one thing.

When a House Is a Hotel

Antoine Nehme at his store circa 1980s.

I have painted a very rosy picture of my youth, but I also must add that there was a lot of anxiety and anger simply because my father was not often at home. He would spend most of his time at work in Qatar or abroad. My mother would, naturally, go crazy. As children, especially for Emil and Simon, it was very rarely that we were able to see him because he was at his office or travelling. Of course, what he was doing was ensuring the future of his family. Quite often, my mother would say to him, "This is not a hotel," when he left early in the morning and returned late in the evening.

He was so taken and busy with work he did not know the names or locations of some of his children's schools!

At times, our home was also a warehouse. We had to relocate several times in a row. One of our houses became, in essence, a storage facility for my father's goods. It came to the point that when guests visited, they had to walk among boxes and crates. Mind you, this was in the front yard. The last straw was when my father brought in a forklift and parked it in the yard. Each time I hear the Arabic word *khallas* (enough),

I remember my mother saying, "Khallas!" as she gave my father a piece of her mind.

As for my sister, Rania, she always had a special place in my father's heart because she was the only daughter. She would sometimes enjoy more freedoms than we boys did. There is no greater relationship than that of a father and his daughter. As close as a father and a son can be, the bond between a daughter and father is something special.

He always called her the "unique one" because she was his only daughter. Raising a daughter was challenging for my parents because my mother was quite progressive and open minded, socially speaking, while Antoine was not so. He worked perfectly in the professional arena, but he was different in society. My parents often clashed over how to raise their children, but they never went to bed angry with each other, which was comforting to my siblings and me.

I can never forget my father's sense of humour. We would be watching TV, and he would burst out laughing at a comedy sketch. His giggling and laughter was quite unique. I remember the question he used to ask me: "Is there anything better than habal?" (*Habal* is Arabic for a silly/ sometimes funny event or object.)

When he was in the right mood, my father loved to socialize and enjoy an evening or a weekend with his inner circle of friends. He would also love to talk and discuss work and would do so with all his children, regularly.

Our family bond was very strong. We went through many things together, including the deaths of many of the older generation. My grandparents started saying goodbye, one after the other. While it was sad and haunting, it was also a uniting force for us children. At the same time, we were raised in a household with a father whom we would nowadays call a workaholic. My siblings and I would come back after these funerals to find our father becoming more and more of a stranger as work absorbed his life. It is hard to think about now, but at times, we would find ourselves asking, "Who is that guy?" when he finally came home after long hours at the office.

In spite of this, I can honestly say I always appreciated him. Indeed, I appreciated him more when I grew older and began to grasp what he did for the business and its day-to-day operations. However, when my father came home, he seemed to fail to realize that we children were not his employees. At times, apparently, he did not realize he was at home. We would tell him, "Dad, we don't work for you." He'd say, "Yes, you work for me." Things would cool down later on after a few tears here and there.

Looking back, I see the humour in some of these stories. My oldest brother, Emil, recalls, "Even at the age of eleven, I was left alone to supervise the store. Even in the early days of the store, I was helping my father mix paints for clients." My other brother, Simon, returned home one day entirely covered in paint. Apparently, he had fallen into a barrel but still had to keep working! This was how rough it was, early on, for my two older brothers as they helped my father build his company, and my mother went berserk with worry over it.

> *"Don't handicap your children by making their lives easy."*
> —*Robert A. Heintein*

Antoine told us something that is important for anyone to think of, no matter where they raise their children: "Children are investments for their parents." We are the future for our parents, and each of us is affected in different ways by our mother and father. Our parents further ensured that we were not too cushioned, as a life of abundance leads to complacency and taking things for granted. It was important for our parents that we grew into the world, finding our way through education. They had faith that an international education would bring new insight, allowing us to better understand where Nehmeh fits in the world at large.

From these humble beginnings, we grew as a company, one with employees of many different nationalities working for it. At first, Antoine focused on importing and did that for nearly forty years. It was not until 1993 that he began to realize that much of what he was importing could be produced in Qatar.

Many of these ideas also came about when my elder brothers began to take on a larger responsibility within the company, bringing back with them knowledge from their international education. My father wanted to make sure we knew more than what he had taught us, and at times, he would test each and every one of us when we came to work for the company. This was especially true for my elder brothers early on. Only when he knew that his investment in his children had worked out, that he could trust us with the company he had founded over four decades before, did he retire, but we will talk about that later.

1990 and the Transition

The year 1990 was a milestone for Emil and Simon. It was the year when my older brothers assumed more responsibility in the family business, after they had graduated from college.

We were all fortunate enough to have been educated all over the world, but we always returned to Qatar, something that baffled many of our friends overseas. They would ask us, "Why are you going back to Qatar? What's in Qatar?" or even, "What is Qatar?"

My older brothers and my sister were continuously travelling and studying, whether in France, Lebanon, or the United States. Still, every summer they would come back to Qatar to work for our father's company.

In 1990 they were fully fledged: they had graduated, and it was thus time to begin work. And that year, both Emil and Simon joined the company, which was still a relatively small venture. Antoine was very excited that they had come and had brought new ideas. My brothers introduced computers and other new technologies. My father did not mind spending money and testing new ways and processes for the company, based on their recommendations. He travelled extensively, leaving the day-to-day operations to my brothers.

My father had once worked with his own brothers. Now, for the first time, he was going to give more responsibilities to his own sons. The situation was new to everyone. For the first time, as they worked with him, all the good and the bad about him would be apparent to them. There was both joy and uncertainty about how this would turn out. Along with these emotions was also the idea of passing the torch to the new generation.

For Antoine, it was absolute joy. He himself was never able to finish college. His children, however, were able to do so thanks to great parents. Here they were, both of his two eldest sons had graduated. For my brothers, I think it was more like, "What are we doing here? We were cruising in Los Angeles, and now, suddenly, we are back in Qatar." Back then, Qatar was not the most exciting or happening place in terms of social nightlife. It was quite difficult for them to grasp what they were getting themselves into.

> *"I am many things all at once: son, husband, and father."*
> —*Antoine Nehme*

There were anxieties and arguments about who should do what because my father had been running the show for decades. When my brothers came, he said, "Okay, you're going to take care of this. You're going to take care of that." That's how delegating particular jobs began, which was important. To think that, seven years later, he would pass on the torch completely is remarkable.

Testing Emil and Simon

Don't give me fish; teach me how to fish

لا تعطيني سمكة لكن علمني كيف اصطاد

It was important for my father to test his children early on. He tested them with stakeholders, banks, governments, institutions, and others who dealt with Nehmeh. He made their lives quite hard to make sure they could work without his supervision. I think he was able to leave them alone because they were two brothers working together. If it had been just one brother, it might not have worked out as easily. With two, it functioned like checks and balances. There is no greater advice than a brother's.

Antoine would, literally, create a crisis out of thin air to test my brothers and observe how they got out of it alone. He would only interfere when it was absolutely required.

One test came about because of the first Gulf War in 1990, soon after my brothers took over the company. I remember the American general's name, Norman Schwarzkopf, often coming up in various conversations and on TV screens at that time.

The war was also called Desert Storm by the American media. It was a very rough time because we were in a state of war and there were missiles flying by and sirens popping up here and there. It was a scary time. Antoine took such news with equanimity, which had a positive affect on us. He remained up to date with the latest events, thanks to his loyal companion, the AM radio that was always by his bedside.

Beyond being tested by war, my brothers sometimes had to determine the financials on their own. They made managerial decisions when they had to call clients and meet them to make sure they were happy. This was all part of my father's continuous process of testing my brothers.

In 1990 I was only about fifteen years old. During my formative teenage years, my father was too busy for me as he worked with my brothers, training them in the ways of the company. He wanted to ensure they were adding value to the family business he had worked so hard to build.

"Don't be afraid to give up the good to go for the great."
—*John D. Rockefeller*

My brothers almost immediately made changes, helping bring the company into the modern era, a process we continue to this day. I remember the new computer systems, for example, a 286 processor, which were advanced for the time. They also used a program from ACCPAC to record and automate processes. It was a revolution for the company—our very first enterprise resource planning software (ERP).

Antoine wanted to learn how to systemize everything. He was always watching Emil and Simon trying to learn the new processes they were bringing into the company, while he simultaneously trained them in the ways of the family business. There was a process and, in a way, the trainer was himself being trained while training others. At the same time, we trained our employees in the new processes while getting them used to the idea that a new generation would be taking over the company. One goal of my brothers that was put forth at the time was to slowly do away with manual processes as much as possible.

The interesting thing was how our founding father had tested and taught his children, while his own goal was to have his children help modernize and expand the business. He was always open to new ideas. He felt that to maintain his edge, he needed the input of new ideas. He was not one to say, "No, we're not going to try that." He was willing to try anything.

Emil is a natural-born salesperson. He has moved up the ranks quite quickly from a sales executive to managing director and has been reelected more than once to a position of chief executive officer by the board of directors. He is on the constant lookout for manufacturers who share our passion for first class customer service and quality. Accordingly, he has added various lines to our portfolio of industrial solutions by listening to customers carefully. He is straightforward and admires efficiency.

As for Simon, he has been the force for various initiatives and reforms and works closely with various authorities to ensure the continued success of many subsidiary companies. He remains key to all the manufacturing activities at Nehmeh. He now spearheads our diversification drive with our new ventures in Qatar and abroad. He champions progressiveness and admires perfectionism and honesty.

More times than not, you are likely to find the son or the daughter of an entrepreneur would inherit such traits and may turn out entrepreneurs themselves.

I remember confronting my father on multiple occasions and telling him that I did not want to be part of his company as I considered it his work, his dream, and his legacy, not mine.

Certainly I was no different from any college kid out there, but that rebellious desire to start on my very own as my father had done with his was indeed restless.

My resistance to work with the company lasted a few years.

I remember him asking me what I wanted to do and how he laughed at my semi-juvenile replies.

Today, I find myself laughing at some of the mad choices I've made too!

I recall the day when he broke through and said to me to go ahead and realize my crazy dreams, but rather than doing so on my own, to do them as part of the company.

While getting my business degree, I was deeply involved in technology before being lured into the family business in late 2001.

With open arms and open books, the company took me in, and I was able to absorb so much knowledge that it would have taken me several years to gather them by myself; my professional learning and understanding was literally fast-tracked.

Today, I am proud to be able to continuously incubate new ventures within Nehmeh.

This is the wisdom you get to notice later on in life, when you engage rather than disconnect from your children in the choices they make, just as my father did with me. Kudos Antoine Nehme.

After learning various programs and holding various positions, I became the service manager and established the after-sales arm of the Nehmeh group. This was comprised of over seventy men and women, engineers, and technicians who took care of all customer feedback, comments, complaints, training, and certification—a group that is referred to today as service solutions.

We introduced leading-edge solutions (some of which have been recognized as firsts in Qatar, the region, and even globally), such as service contracts, a service hotline, online service, live online service tracking.

This is the after-sales market, which is a component of our commitment to our clients and a part of our commitment to a journey with our customers that continues long after the original purchase.

Currently, I also lead the Strategic Initiatives Office (SIO), which controls and directs various long-term objectives, as set by the board of directors, with a goal of enhancing business structure and processes of Nehmeh. As an agent of change, my role is to facilitate smooth transitions within the organization.

My shared-services responsibilities include the following departments at the group level: administration, human resources, IT, and marketing (including corporate communications).

Rania came into the company in 2006, and she quickly demonstrated an exceedingly intelligent approach to running the company.

In the early 1990s, when Emil and Simon began to run the company, Rania was still studying in France and later in Canada. When she joined the company, she joined as an equal, which was revolutionary back then simply because women were not always treated that way in Middle Eastern companies. In Qatar, the workforce was dominated by men, but slowly, with greater awareness and the efforts of Sheikh Hamad bin Khalifah Al Thani's consort, Sheikha Moza bint Nasser Al Missned, as well as other leading women from the ruling family, social changes began to occur.

Times have definitely now changed, including in Qatar. What was important, though, is that my sister brought in a way of thinking that was quite different from that of my brothers. This was because Rania was the only one in the family who had worked outside the family business before joining us. She had earned her degrees and her MBA, which added real value, especially to human resources. For the first time, we set up an HR department. In the past, employees were often dealt with somewhat randomly—in a nondocumented manner. Now, we had solid HR systems and procedures.

Continuing to Pass the Torch

We know that the company will continue to evolve after our current management. We already have a new generation finishing college. They are our children, my father's grandchildren. Among them are young people in their early twenties, just finishing their university education.

As do the branches on a tree, we all grow in different directions, yet our roots remain as one. Additionally, we have had a smooth transition, and we will ensure this will be the case for these future generations. We have learned lessons from different families and enjoy the invaluable business continuity left by our founding father. When he passed away in 2010, we were, maybe, one of the few families who had no inheritance issues.

This was very farsighted and modern. We thought about these transitions as long ago as 2002, when we started asking ourselves what we would do for our own children. The corporate evolution continues. We are currently in the middle of a restructure allowing us to continue making such smooth transitions.

We are very transparent about this within the company and outside the company. More than once, we have been invited to share our story in various regional family business conferences. I discuss and showcase how we are moving from a traditional to a modern corporate structure. I explain that we are ensuring the company lives on, well beyond our lives.

We owe it to ourselves, and we owe it to our history to preserve our name, to preserve our family, to preserve our business, and of course, to continue to uphold our esteem and loyalty to Qatar. Our family name is our company name. This means we have a huge responsibility. We are always wary not to jeopardize our name or our position for the sake of both the family and the company. It is something we owe to each other, to our clients, to our staff, and most importantly, to the country of Qatar, which has nourished us to become the business force we are today.

CHAPTER 6

Education and Values: The Importance of Solid Foundations

"Education is not the filling of a pail, but rather the lighting of a fire."

—*W. B. Yeats*

My father taught his children and his employees the value of education, moulding a new generation. We children were educated all over the world, bringing international experience to the company. Learning from abroad was important for all of us personally and for its impact on the company. We were educated in a diverse range of places including renowned institutions in France, the United States, Canada, and schools in Lebanon and Qatar.

I believe Antoine's appreciation of the value of education stems from his not being able to fulfil his own personal educational wishes because of the hardships he lived through. He used to say, "People can take away everything from you. They can take away your clothes, your watch, your shoes, but they can never take away your education. They can never take away your brain."

You must also remember that he was, in some ways, a refugee many times over, forced to leave the places where he had lived. This included being forced to flee from Palestine in 1948 and being forced to leave Lebanon for economic reasons in 1953. These difficult events cemented for him the importance of education. He did not spare a dime educating his children at universities and colleges across the world. The schools where we were educated were not the online or multi-country campus institutions of today. You needed to travel to them and reside there.

For my father, the cost of educating his children was a sacrifice he was willing to take. He was also in total alignment with my mother in this view of education as the most important thing. At home, you learn values; you learn morals and what is right and what is wrong. Once you are exposed to the world, education is a tool to help you go it alone.

My parents also realized their own mortality. They figured education was one way of maintaining their legacy. What better way than having educated children? Later, we children worked hard to keep educating not just our own children but also our company employees.

The Children and Their Studies

"May God shield you from hardships."
— *Antoine Nehme*

Emil and Simon studied all over the world, from being among the first children to enroll in the first French school in Qatar, to studying in Lebanon, France, and the United States. One graduated in marketing while the other graduated in management. Rania's education was in Lebanon, France, and Canada.

Emil studied for his executive MBA at HEC Paris. The "HEC" stands for Hautes Études Commerciales (Advanced Business Studies). The school is among the most important business schools in the world. Rania earned a degree from the Sorbonne University in France to the University of Montréal in Canada and later continued her education, gaining an MBA at the École Supérieure des Affaires (Superior Business School) in Beirut, Lebanon.

As for myself, I had the pleasure and luxury of studying in Qatar, Lebanon, and Canada at various institutions and earning my long-sought-after degree in management information systems.

Naturally, education being a journey rather than a destination, the schooling never ends, and I continued with various courses at INSEAD and other reputable universities and business schools.

Long before we began our advanced education around the world, we had all been educated overseas. We had, for instance, received some of our grade school education in France, for several years during the 1980s when we lived there. We returned to Qatar, as a family, in 1986, with Emil and Simon returning in 1990, following their higher education. Rania was also in France in 1990. Then, in 1993, I moved to Canada for my education and finally finished my various degrees in 2003.

We were never forced by my father to follow any particular field of study while receiving our degrees. He used to say, "Do whatever the heck you want." He did not impose anything on us other than a plea to learn. He left us with our own free will. Rania, for example, studied history for many years. Then she continued with a bachelor's degree in business and a master's in business as well. As for me, I did computer science and business management. It was, again, laissez-faire because my father figured there would always be something to be brought back into the company. We did indeed have that freedom.

There is also no greater joy for parents than to have all their children graduate from university. My parents felt a lot of pride and were pleased that their sacrifices had finally paid off. Their children were experiencing a classic life in which children grow up, go to school and university, travel the world, get married, have kids of their own, and so on. My parents were happy that this classic progression was followed by all of us. It was, in essence, a circle of life and provided some sort of closure for them.

I think if Antoine had been asked to repeat the 1950s all over again, he would have done it in a heartbeat. Whereas he made investments on behalf of his parents, his brothers, and his sisters, he would now invest in his children's education. This is a beautiful gesture and a reminder of what a kind human being he was. That spirit of giving remained unchanged throughout his life.

At the same time, we can never forget the role my mother played during the period when we were being educated. While my father was working, my mother was the one doing the travelling and checking up on her children, no matter where we were in the world.

Interestingly, many children sent off from our part of the world would head to the West and, somehow, secretly marry. Fortunately, this was not the case for us. However, there were stories of parents sending their kids off to college far away and not being aware that their children had had children or that they had gotten married secretly, unknowingly and likely against their parents' wishes. Many people from our region began living secret lives as soon as they went to study in the West. They never shared their lives with their parents, which caused a lot of heartache.

We were not like this. Instead, for us, there was a weekly phone call every Sunday or so, just to stay in touch. It was an appointment. Cellular and mobile phones were still experimental back then. To the extent that he could, depending on his business responsibilities, my father would travel back and forth to visit us. He would fly from Qatar to join up with us and spend a few days—or vacation time, if he was also travelling for his work. The times when we are away from our family are much harder. Because we're not always in touch, we wonder what has happened to our family during the past two, three, or six months, and that uncertainty becomes an emotional burden. On the other hand, that yearning to see and hear a person or enjoy a moment with loved ones creates something wonderful: appreciation. But the ability to reroute ourselves to the here and now is also a blessing in its own right.

"To be upset over what you don't have is to waste what you do have."
—*Ken S. Keyes*

We live in an age when we take immediate communication for granted. If somebody doesn't reply to your instant message within two minutes, you begin to worry. Before all these communication apps and devices, we had something called patience. We waited. You had to hold your breath for weeks on end. Communication was mainly through the telephone and those ever-colourful postcards. How different communication was at that time is important for young people to understand. We simply do not have the barriers we used to have. It was so expensive to use the phone. Time was so valuable you had to make sure you got the right feelings across quickly without any misunderstanding.

When talking to your parents, especially, in those precious minutes on a long-distance phone call, you had to reassure them you were alive and well. All of that was not easy. Understandably, during those moments, patience was a virtue for all students studying abroad. But there was always this constant craving for more: "I wish I could speak more, but I can't. I wish I could express more, but I am not able." It taught you to be more appreciative of time management and emotional intelligence, more so than many of our peers are today.

It is also important to point out that those of us growing up in Qatar had to leave the country to get a proper higher education. Being away was difficult yet necessary. As Qatar was a developing nation, higher education of any type was not readily available there. And for us, our educational choice was between North America and Europe. There was not much of an option really.

Nowadays things are very different. Doha is a city full of educational opportunity at every level, including local campuses of various Ivy League American institutions and other renowned European institutions.

When you went away to college, one of two things would happen: (1) from your solid platform you would shine, entering adulthood with flying colours, or (2) you could fail because of a pampered, somewhat spoiled upbringing.

Remember, as a small, wealthy country, Qatar provided a privileged environment to all the people who walked its soil. This fortunate upbringing could make one lose appreciation of basic things—including effort!

The assistance at home (maids and nannies) was even available on the road. Literally everything could be delivered to your automobile—after you sounded your car horn twice—without your ever needing to step out of your vehicle.

You could be called presumptuous, perhaps—assuming you felt entitled to be treated like royalty, with everyone calling you "sir."

Children may lose their way, sometimes more than once, but in the arms of their parents, they cannot help but tell them what they are going through as they may be the only people who have your best interest at heart and who will love you no matter what. Even if it is going to break their parents' heart, you tell them how it is.

We were very lucky to have been nurtured in a home where telling the truth was encouraged and appreciated. It was not something to be afraid of. We would not lie to one another. That home was a very special refuge, a special members-only haven.

When you are young and leave a conservative environment for a more liberal one, you may get carried away. Coming from a conservative society where you lived within a shell of protectionism, strange things may happen because you have not experienced this kind of freedom before. It is natural for all children to let loose too much when away from parental controls, and for those of us from conservative environments, this is even more of a temptation.

That was something my parents were not afraid of because they ensured that we were, very early on, exposed as much as possible to the ways of the world. Certainly, no childhood is perfect, but when a child goes astray, a great family comes together—not to blame, shame, or disown but to show strength. There is no greater love than that.

Additionally, our global education meant that we could understand multiple languages, including our three basic languages of Arabic, French, and English, with which we have been familiar since childhood. That helped the company a lot. Being Lebanese is a tremendous multicultural advantage throughout the world. Lebanon is first and foremost a Mediterranean country, and so we were exposed to Mediterranean languages and cultures. Historically, we Lebanese have always had a "light tongue," so we could speak with ease in any language. Many Lebanese speak Arabic as easily as Portuguese or Bulgarian, or several other languages, for that matter.

We went even further and tried other languages, including Spanish, German, and Japanese. Arabic, English, and French remain our pillars. Those are three languages that we all share. Every new language you learn opens a new culture. I believe the British singer Tom Jones once said he loved people who have accents. That means they know another language, which makes them more interesting all together.

*"Education is the most powerful weapon which you can use
to change the world."*
—Nelson Mandela

At the heart of it, the educational process was part of passing the business from one generation to the next. Even though the passing of the torch began in 1990, the process began a lot earlier. The root of our business education began with store and factory visits when we were all very young.

Following on from such visits, which taught us what my father knew, we were encouraged to seek out education as broadly as possible throughout the world. That exposure helped us work really great wonders because it taught us new ideas and that not everything we do is necessarily the correct way, be it in daily life or at work. For me to see countries and cities that had enjoyed stability for a long time or that had long established a working, solid system of government was mind expanding to the point where I felt a bit intimidated at first by the wow factor— namely, that there is so much to life.

When you study abroad, you also study the people around you. You have to live among the locals. On the one hand, the experience tests you. On the other hand, you learn much that you can take back with you. How open is your home or business to new ideas?

The whole act of travelling was just incredible. We were so far away from friends and family that we learned to be independent. And we ensure that our own children are also exposed to many different ideas and languages.

"The world hates change, yet it is the only thing that has brought progress."
—*Charles F. Kettering*

It is very important not to stereotype people. I like to think that my siblings and I have that same open-mindedness that our parents had. They were, paradoxically, quite traditional but, thankfully, progressive. They knew that old ways cannot last forever. Some things need to change. You either embrace that change, or you sit on the side and decay.

Even though being separated from their children—scattered, as we were, all over the world—was difficult for my parents, they embraced it as a natural progression of life.

Identity

Expatriates (often shortened to the word *expats*) are those who live outside their native country.

In time, you acquire a tag of "allegiance" to the country you have spent the most time in, which is normal for many expatriates around the world.

As a family, we may carry various nationalities, however, we are Lebanese citizens. We are Arabs and speak Arabic as our mother tongue.

Why does this matter? Well, if we do not have a clear sense of who we really are, we may struggle with an emotional fallout. This can result in the disruption or an all-out loss of relationships with a country or its people.

Nonetheless, some of us may consider ourselves as "citizens of the world," which is perhaps a classic expatriate statement nowadays.

Apart from gaining expanded horizons and knowledge, I believe people who think of themselves as global citizens turn out, for the most part, to be the most objective, thoughtful, rational, open-minded, and experienced people.

By retaining our values and beliefs, we never let go of who we truly are, and our sense of appreciation for such traits only grows stronger.

Certainly, such diversity is an enriching experience for us and those around us, and this clearly manifests itself at Nehmeh.

An Education at Factories

How does that relate to the original business my father developed? It created a sense of independence and courage and an ability to say, "No. I'm going to make my own decision. I'm going to be up to the task. I will bear the consequences; good or bad." Our curiosity, however, started when we were much smaller, going on those factory visits. We used to wonder how things were made. We got the answer by visiting factories.

Those visits became a sort of hobby for us. Just as our founding father liked to listen to an orchestra and watch the conductor synchronizing all the musicians, we like to listen to the noise of a machine and guess which machines are running from the noise they make. We like to visit factories as much as possible, even if there is no immediate need to do so.

As educated as we have become, we understand the human miracle of fabricating something with our own hands. This is the essence of a factory, though the process may be more mechanical and more on an assembly line basis. No matter how many academic degrees we have, none of us loses sight of this understanding, which has proven an important element in our latest ventures into the hospitality and restaurant businesses, which share similar principles.

Our open-mindedness while being mindful of tradition may be seen as a Lebanese value. Historically, Lebanese immigrants tend to do very well in their new homes across the world. We find this to be the case whether we have been uprooted because of our own civil war from 1975 to 1990 or because of conflicts in neighbouring countries, which unfortunately continue to this day. Somehow, Lebanese immigrants tend to be better at advancing themselves than other immigrants. We know how to overcome adversity in our struggles to make a new life. This sense of survival is innate.

I think we can summarize it for the Nehme family as follows: We have a good mix of more than one element. It is not a continuum or something with only two sides. It is more of a square coaster. On one edge, we have conservatism. On another edge, we have our values and open-mindedness. On the third edge, we have protectionism, and on the fourth edge, we have risk taking.

Our home in the Gulf provided the platform for my father and his family to truly expand their horizons. Added to this was a constant exposure to innovation and a constant avalanche of ideas, visits, travels, and welcoming others into our circle. This means we cannot pin the main reason for doing so well solely on the fact that we are a Lebanese family. All of these factors came together to make it happen, and Qatar especially helped us with all the opportunities it provided.

Of course, we also made sure we were open to those opportunities, and they, in turn, helped to expand our own view on life—on this I speak on behalf of my brothers and sister as well as for myself. It is an important fact.

As a Lebanese, I will allow myself to criticize the society to which I belong. After all, a sense of humour includes being able to laugh at oneself, doesn't it? The joke is Lebanese expatriates do fantastically well in their personal life and business outside Lebanon, while Lebanese living in Lebanon do not do so well. Why this is so may demand a full chapter in a future book.

It is for these reasons that Qatar has been and continues to be a wonderful place for many of the Nehme family to call home.

CHAPTER 7

Loyalty: Keeping and Delivering on Promises

"One must marry one partner at home and at work: one wife, one bank"

—*Antoine Nehme*

Loyalty and the sense of belonging are very important to us in the Nehme family. We feel we have a message to send across. When we deliver this message, we want it to have substance. We do not talk or brag about something we do not understand or have no experience with. We talk about and work with what we know.

We always like to say we love our people. If you search "Nehmeh people" online, you will be taken to our website. Right there, on the second line, you can read what gives us great pride: that we love our people!

As long as you show strength, people will not merely follow you; they will become your advocates. It is a much more important relationship than that between a leader and a follower. We love to involve our people in our company's decision-making process. When we achieve something significant, as a company, we send out a post so that our people know. We also ask them about potential changes with questions such as "What do you think of this new plan?"

After all, we are still a private business. We are not in the public sector, nor are we registered on the stock market. We are under no obligation to disclose any type of information. Still, we feel it is necessary to share some information with our people. Rather than giving numbers, we give percentages. We say we are up this much. We are down this much. We are doing that. We are exploring this. We are investing in that.

The key is to communicate. We communicate with our people as much as possible in order to keep our work exciting. We think it keeps the workplace in motion. There is always something new brewing.

Most importantly, we have a vision for our company, and we share that with our people. That was something we worked very, very hard on. We worked as a team of fifteen managers sitting together to figure out this great company's vision back in 2013.

Our vision is simple and yet powerful: to become a regional key player committed to delivering innovative excellence through sustainable and diversified businesses by 2020.

Our vision excites people. It makes people impatient too because a lot of people say, "Come on already. We want to see change. Let's change now. Let's do this." We are also a company in transition, moving from a family-run model to a more corporate structure, as we expand. While we make that move, we know that we have to have a lot of heart. We have to be empathetic to the needs of our employees. For that reason, we have an open-door policy, making ourselves constantly available to them.

I personally lead the change management at Nehmeh. In many ways, as one of the leadership team, you become the local shrink or the local doctor to your staff. Should you succeed once, twice, three times, you create a following. You create this great loyalty.

We like loyalty, but we also know that not everyone can be loyal to the company. If people are not loyal by nature, if they are people who cheat their friends or spouses, more often than not, we are likely to see such people will end up cheating the business as well. What we look for are real values. We are one of those companies that ask strange questions when hiring. You could be the most professionally qualified person, but if we find, when we do a background check, that you have morality issues or come from a dysfunctional family and have not recovered from that bad experience, we consider your personal problems may work against the company and against The Nehmeh Way.

We need a near-perfect marriage early on. We do not want to get to the point where we are married and, one week later, realize we made a mistake and seek a divorce. Instead, we put new hires on probation. In interviews, we make sure to ask about the candidate's mother and father, and we perform rigorous background checks. We are not extremists when it comes to our hiring process, but we would like our code, The Nehmeh Way, to be respected and upheld.

It is not because it has worked in the past and it is going to continue working. Not at all. It is because this is what we stand for. This is what we wake up for every morning. When we talk about the core values of people, the quality, the trust, the commitment, this is who we are. This is what we do as individuals, as a family, and as a company. For those of us behind the Nehmeh brand and the Nehme family, it is very important to keep sending these messages, as that is what builds confidence in our staff and in our clients.

We know also that while we seek people with values, we also have to help build values as well. As an example, when children start to ride a bicycle, they have training wheels. When you leave them to ride on their own, they hesitate. You run after them. And you push. The second you let go, it's the classic Kodak moment. You let them go, and they ride away successfully. That is the leap of faith you should achieve with your employees. Once you let them go, you empower them to either fall or continue cycling. This is a defining moment. Still, if the attempt fails, it is okay to try again.

This is how you build a following. We are not trying to build a cult like the kind you might find in some companies. Instead, we are trying to build a corporate culture that is a place for openness, respect, and appreciation. Not only do we work under the shadow of the founder, but we are a part of his continuing legacy.

A close family environment also means we have a very high retention of employees, which we know has positive and negative aspects. Of course, it is positive in the sense that we receive incredible loyalty from our staff, and we are loyal to our staff in return. These are people who have been with us through many different events and economic, commercial, and operational crises. They know the history of the company, and the company knows theirs.

At the same time, there can be negative aspects, such as a certain complacency that we work hard to overcome. There may be employees who watch clocks rather than work. In this sense, I think it is important for a company to recreate itself. These employees must be given a chance to recreate themselves with proper guidance and management. It is terrific when it works out. However, if employees still cannot recreate themselves after training, we believe it is best for them to look elsewhere for employment.

A Diverse Group

As a diverse company, with employees from around the world, many regions are represented: the Middle East, Asia, Europe, and North and South America. As a member of the leadership team, I am honoured to attract—and keep attracting—such diverse and amazing candidates who choose to work with us and become a part of the Nehmeh family.

How do we do it? We do what many other companies do. For instance, we find people through mainstream methods such as online business recruitment websites. We put candidates through a process with multiple interviews. We interview the same candidate perhaps three or four times, not just to compare notes but also to make sure that person knows what we are about as a company.

We check background references. Most importantly, at the candidate's place of employment, we check their reputation and reasons for leaving. Many times, we travel to the candidate's home country. We don't just meet that candidate, but we make it a point to meet other candidates as well. This gives us a pool of people from which to select our final choice.

During the interview, we also share our story. This is as much about us getting to know the interviewees as it is about them getting to know us. We tell them this is who we are. This is where we come from in terms of history and heritage, and this is where we are going. We take note of the candidates' reactions. Some will be excited. The intriguing thing we find is that for some people, it does not seem to matter if a company is sixty years old or sixty days old. We are in an age of start-ups, but for me, personally, as a consumer and as a potential employee, I would want to know that I am joining a company that is secure and stable. There is much to be said about a company that has been around for sixty years.

A Stable Family Business

> *"Motivation is a fire from within. If someone else tries to light that fire under you, chances are it will burn very briefly."*
> —Stephen R. Covey

We are working hard towards corporate governance and restructuring our way of doing things. What is important for us, as the founding family, is to keep the momentum of the company going, especially through this latest transition.

Keeping up the momentum means that when we hire people, there will be excitement that they are joining our company, whether in Qatar or elsewhere. We make it a point to showcase how well we treat our people, and they always want to see that the company is on the move. We say, "Yes, this company is indeed a family business first. Yet we are currently restructuring." It has already started. There is no going back.

There are also positive changes on how decisions are made. This helps new employees relax a bit. We also maintain continuity through internal candidates, helping them move up within the company along a career path. There is, perhaps, no greater pleasure for me than watching the employees I have worked with over the years move up through the ranks. I believe that such employees are also among the most positive role models for both clients and potential new employees.

"Positivity is contagious: either you affect people or infect people."
—*Unknown*

Such employees are perhaps the best spokespeople for our company—better than a public relations agency. We wish to reach such a level with all our staff and clients that they become more a team of advocates than simply a following.

We imagine our people being asked if they would recommend working at Nehmeh. We work to hear a definitive, genuine yes. We would like to know that they recognize and understand that this company has direction, has the tools and the means, and knows where it's going. Having a team of happy employees is like having a well-tuned orchestra at one's command, always ready to play in harmony. As one of the company's leaders, and moreover, as a family member, I believe team effort ensures things happen and the company moves ahead.

*"The achievements of an organization
are the results of the combined effort of each individual."*
—*Vince Lombardi*

When we say we have a vision and values, it is not a template that we copied and pasted. Our values are as timeless, as they are really boundless. The questions we know our employees ask themselves and can say yes to include whether the company respects employees as persons, whether it offers quality jobs, whether it is a quality firm, whether employees are trusted to make decisions, and whether the company commits to its employees and fulfils its promises.

As long as you do not lie to your people and as long as you live by what you preach—doing what you say and saying what you do—you can do anything as a company and you will earn the trust of the people. You need that firm confidence, and once you have it, you can do anything. You must have a firm belief that nothing will shake your ground.

CHAPTER 8

Sustainability: What It Really Means

"If you don't keep a close eye on your wealth, someone else will."

—Antoine Nehme

`At Nehmeh, sustainability is more than just a buzzword or something to plaster into advertising as the latest public-relations fad. On the contrary, long before it was fashionable, we believed strongly in sustainability for the employees and the environment. We believe it is a key value for the maintenance of the company and for the benefit of all stakeholders.

Why do we believe in these things? It all has to do with the security of the company, our workers, and our clients. This gives an added value to the company and to everything we do. At the end of the day, who better knows the business than the people who have been with it through thick and thin, through the good times and the bad?

It is our people who help us maintain the values that will sustain the company into the future. In essence, these people are family, the sons and daughters of the broader Nehmeh family. I might be part of the founding family, but we have employees who pre-date me and my siblings. They are part of how we sustain the company. I sometimes feel they have been here forever and will be here until the day they die. This is something we take pride in, and we find absolute joy in welcoming individuals who are second-generation employees. Imagine, the father worked here, and he entrusted Nehmeh to a level that he is willing to send his own children to work here, too.

> *"Keep an eye on your work, for if you neglect it,*
> *it will feel it and neglect you in return."*
> —Antoine Nehme

We have many such examples of loyal employees. These are people we hold on our shoulders as models for our employees and our prospective employees.

"If you are sad, the company will be sad.
If you are happy, the company will be happy."
—Antoine Nehme

We believe in the concept of letting go, which means passing the torch to other people who may be more qualified than ourselves because of their experience, education, or another credential. We do this through delegation and empowerment.

As we develop Nehmeh from a family-run business into a more corporate model, the concept of letting go can be rather difficult. To a degree, it is like walking down the aisle with your child during a marriage ceremony. That child eventually becomes an adult man or woman. Giving your child away is like the analogy of a bicycle with training wheels. You let the child go, but it requires a little faith. Whether via a marriage or via teaching a child to ride a bicycle, we must all learn to let our people go on their own. That same principle applies to family businesses.

No matter what checks and balances and committees may have been set up for our transition, we always have a fear of jeopardizing the company name in some way. If we are unable to eliminate the errors and shocks that might occur during the transition, we want to at least minimize them.

We would like to reach the point where we family members withdraw more and more from the business operation, which will still be family owned, but we want to ensure it operates well. We have come to learn more about this process through the many seminars and conferences in which we participate. We have learned that while people who founded companies may die, the companies can continue to thrive. Being here and writing this book for you is testimony to this and to the person who founded this great company. We know that we will be here sixty years into the future and beyond. This is a major component of our belief in sustainability.

"Wisdom is knowing what to do next.
Skill is knowing how to do it. Virtue is doing it."
—David Starr Jordan

To succeed in sustainability, we have to change the mind-set of the stake-holders. As one of them, I know this can be tough to absorb. On the other hand, we could very well continue without changing. No harm would be done. The company would still uphold its reputation and generate revenue. However, this is shortsighted, as it is unsustainable and will eventually lead to the disappearance of the company all together.

Naturally, for the benefit of all the stakeholders, we try to always hire those who match the profile of our group to ensure that we talk the talk and walk the walk. As part of our motto, we use the words "trusted partner," but we use them with great care and make sure we deliver on our promises. We always say that we are your partner in business. We are not just there as a provider, a seller, or a reseller. We will be with you throughout the life cycle of your business, providing you with veritable solutions based on both your timeline and budget.

Bringing Our Values to a Global Level

"Wherever there is a human being, there is an opportunity for kindness."
—Lucius Annaeus Seneca

It became apparent that we had to take care of our own people. To do so, once again our values were called in. More importantly, we joined a voluntary network of the United Nations called Global Compact

(UNGC). This project has helped us with our sustainability goals and more importantly, with broader ethical and environmental issues that we believe in and that go far beyond our own business needs, including human rights, labour rights, voluntary sustainability, and a green emphasis on how we do business.

The vision of the UNGC is to increase loyalties and to end poverty and suffering. How do you mix these objectives with the goal of a business, which is simply to make money? One method is to provide more than just handouts. A lot of the so-called sustainability we see around us is just for show. For example, a factory might be making the effort to save paper while continuing to pollute the environment behind the scenes.

We dare to take initiatives that many other companies do not. For instance, in the case of the UNGC, our partnership began as a result of our approaching the UN. We first learned of the initiative from one of our own vendors, a much larger company. It was something I was immediately struck by and curious to learn more about. Importantly, we found out that the initiative covered labour laws and other aspects of human rights that aligned with Qatar's vision.

Being a part of the UN initiative is a result of our constant craving for knowledge. It is also an example of our own initiative in which we seek out ways to help others and to become a part of the world around us. We see an opportunity, and we seize it.

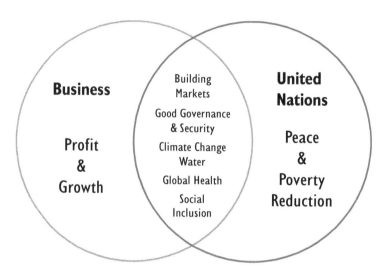

We wanted more than a stamp of approval for signing up and more than letters from Ban Ki-moon, the secretary general of the United Nations. So we have published our endeavours. We wanted our records to incorporate a communication of progress (COP). This annually updated and released document shows what our company is doing on four different fronts: labour rights, human rights, environment, and anticorruption. These four issues are very dear to me on a personal level.

When we talk about labour rights, the question is how we treat our own people. Human rights are not only about how you treat people but what you give them and what you make available to them. The work environment, a used and abused phrase, is key to this concept. The issues are self-explanatory and include not just offering employees a nonhazardous place of work but also a healthy, comfortable, safe place of work. In addition, of course, our business operates in a transparent manner and is not involved in any unethical acts, thus upholding the anticorruption component of the initiative. These are all integral to the Nehmeh way.

WE SUPPORT

The official logo of United Nations Global Compact supporters.

The compliance process was rigorous, but we did it, and we've been doing it since 2012. It is not another trophy for us but rather a way of putting our neck on the line by announcing that these values are what we stand for. Are we up to the job? It keeps everybody on their toes, allowing us to re-examine our processes. Whenever we do something, we make sure beforehand that what we have signed up for corresponds with what we stand for. The company values then become a mix of internal and external values that, fortunately, align. With this UN agreement we are exposing our values and processes to the world. I invite you to check the process and our compliance for yourself by going online at https://www.unglobalcompact.org/what-is-gc/participants/17242.

Our Commitment to Doing Good

"The generous is given in abundance while the selfish is taken from."
—Antoine Nehme

My father was very kind and extremely generous. One story I remember was about my mother getting upset with him because he would often come home without a shirt; he'd simply be bare-chested. She would ask, "Antoine, where are your clothes?" His simple answer would be, "I gave them away. One fellow needed a shirt, so I gave it away." He gave away many things, from shirts to watches to vehicles. He always believed in the creed, "If God has given you much, make sure you give much back in return."

It is this selfless philosophy that has also led us, as a family, to set up a registered, independent, nongovernmental, nonpolitical, nonprofit, civil society organization with the name of Antoine Nehme Foundation (http://antoine.nehme.foundation). Working along with its partners, the foundation's mantra is "helping people help themselves." The vision is to achieve a just and secure society through moral and financial inter-dependence and cooperation. It was founded in honour of Antoine Nehme after his passing and continues his work to make sure the society that helped him continues to flourish and that above all, no one goes to bed hungry as Antoine and members of his family had to do so many decades ago.

Antoine Nehme Foundation, a nonprofit civil society organization.

We always say that one of our philosophies is "doing good while doing well." By that, we mean we might be good at making money, but we also have to give back. At the end of the day, we are expatriates living in a foreign land. This is where we are, and we intend to give back to all the communities we serve. In many ways this is a reminder of how good Qatar and other countries have been in helping us, as an immigrant family, to become successful.

"We make a living by what we get, but we make a life by what we give."
—*Winston Churchill*

It is perhaps easier in one's own country to help maintain a roadside garden or help the homeless person on the street or join the neighbourhood watch or support the local football team. Living and working in a country that is not your own makes things a little bit harder. We give back to our community by being a bit more creative. We have our local, semiprofessional, expatriate basketball, football, and cricket teams. We fund their games as well as provide them with uniforms.

Additionally, when we know we can help our own expatriate workers in greater depth, we do so.

Be it the recent floods in the Far East, the quakes on the Indian subcontinent, or the wars in the Middle East, we work together with our staff of all nationalities to raise funds in collaboration with local charities. Nehmeh always matches the total contributions raised for such causes to double the impact and do our part in bettering the world.

We do this within our means as a small-to-medium-sized company. We do not have the rich resources and enormous army of staff to call upon to take care of things, as do our behemoth counterparts. It is vital to be wary of going overboard.

Our company's transition involves creating several autonomous, small, business units that are able to perform a variety of functions. It is not only that everything we're doing is because of what we have been given; we also need to credit our people who are working hard every single day, which I must admit is hard work in itself as we honour the new generation we are welcoming into Nehmeh. This generation includes those who began to work for the company after the founding father had passed on.

We look at sustainability as a second opportunity, one we want to make sure to seize. We do not allow ourselves to fall back on our laurels and become comfortable with the status quo. We have decided to do much more than this. We appreciate that we have achieved a great deal as a company and as the family that founded the company. We have a great sense of gratitude, while at the same time, we have a greater sense of responsibility.

As members of the founding family and a new generation running the company, we must continuously earn our positions. This creates an incredible drive within us to make things even better. Squandering such wonderful opportunities for progress would not be right. This is why it is important for us to grow—and grow right.

Sustainability is not just to maintain a profit margin and revenue growth. No, my friends, sustainability is also the belief in giving back. Let's say you have been given a particular freedom, fortune, or advantage. There's an invoice somewhere for that—spiritual, mental, or physical. It needs to be paid somewhere, sometime, somehow. Each of us has an invoice that we owe to the greater world, whether we see it in a spiritual or in a secular sense.

Perhaps the phrase, "I paid my dues" applies here in the non-financial meaning. We must always pay our dues. It is about the obligations we have to each other and to society as a whole.

The Environment and the New Generation

Even when my father founded the company, I know he always thought of others and the larger world into which he fit. It is for this reason that he was so grateful to Qatar for the opportunities the country gave him.

Yet there were certain things that men of his generation did not think of as often as we do in this generation. Among them is the impact of business on the environment. It is for this reason, as we prepare to pass the company on to the new generation, that we are adding environmental principles to our processes. These principles were not necessarily of concern in the 1950s when the company was founded. As part of the progression of the company, this concern about the environment as the company grows and expands is the responsibility of my generation and those that will follow.

We feel that care for our environment is a moral duty. We have seen how far we have pushed our environment. As a company, we also know that we have been ahead of our time in that regard as many of our initiatives in environmental matters pre-date environmental laws. We always did pursue these initiatives, voluntarily, because we collectively felt it necessary.

We know other companies do such things as well. Yet we have often found they do not take action out of genuine concern but rather to attract media attention and for the purpose of public relations. In our case, we take action because we want it to be known that this is who we are. Even if a new generation of leaders from outside the Nehme family takes over the helm, we want to make sure they uphold this value. It is in this way that Nehmeh does things. Nehmeh cares about these things because the Nehme family cares about them.

Developing countries often need a better way of doing things. We know that as countries and companies grow, they have to find their own way to methods that, perhaps, Europe and the United States learned long ago, during their own early growing spurts. Development can itself create abuses and increasingly requires laws that were not necessary in the past. You simply cannot fast-forward legislation and dictate that changes that took hundreds of years to evolve in the West are adopted by developing countries in a matter of a few years.

At the same time, sacrifices have to be made, and they will be made, more often than not, against some people's will and convenience. One of our values, however, is our people. Treating people well is an important part of our company's sustainability program.

I believe sustainability will be more and more important because we simply cannot keep doing what we are doing, as a human race, and not pay the invoice. Earth, the environment, the people, the families—they have a price to pay. Unless businesses act responsibly, we will have a difficult time enforcing sustainability laws and environmental decrees. Agencies, government departments, and ministries must come together to protect not just the environment but the people in that environment as well.

I caution those running companies not to close their eyes or hide behind the issues because the environment is too important. For us, sustainability is a natural transition to the legacy we maintain. What is it that you, as a company leader, want to maintain? As we transition from a traditional family structure to a corporate one, sustainability is one aspect of how we maintain our livelihood.

Our employees, whether Omar, Emmanuel, or Miriam, will automatically become Omar Nehmeh, Emmanuel Nehmeh, and Miriam Nehmeh. We baptize them in our own name. This is not in a religious way, of course—all our employees are free to worship however they wish—but we welcome them to their new extended family. Sustainability is simply doing right by the company and by our employees.

We also believe part of our sustainability involves doing right by each other. The fact that when our founding father passed on, the family had zero inheritance issues is something we do not take lightly. This is also a major component of sustainability. At Nehmeh, we work together to make things easier, better, and smoother—for each other and for those who work with us. This is sustainability too.

Using our vision as a beacon, we began our diversification drive a few years ago and entered new industries.

This has the triple purpose of (1) following the vision, (2) diversifying the portfolio, and (3) making the Nehmeh group more attractive for the new generation of employees.

Yet, we remain on the lookout for partners who share our passion for first-class customer service and expect this diversification to continue with new activities in the years to come.

CHAPTER 9

Legacy: Reflections on the Past as We Look Ahead

"The things you do for yourself are gone when you are gone,
but the things you do for others remain as your legacy."
—*Kalu Ndukwe Kalu*

It is time, once again, for us to begin thinking of passing the torch here at Nehmeh. The mechanics are in place for the transition to flow smoothly as we move from generation to generation and into our new corporate structure.

One of the biggest shocks for our company came in the 1990s in the form of an economic crisis during our first leadership transition.

Money in Qatar was tight at this difficult time. Still, the family was growing, along with the number of staff. We were expanding in spite of the national situation. The fact remains, though, that it was a difficult period for Emil, Simon, and my father, who were running things then. Not only did they have to tighten their belts, but they also had to find new ways to do things. They needed to simplify processes and make it easier for other companies to work with us. Businesses were in a very conservative mode when it came to spending money. And yet, we survived this.

Through the years.

"When the winds of change blow,
some people build walls and others build windmills."
—Chinese Proverb

We say the company can withstand whatever shock is thrown at it, and to some people this might seem a cliché. Yet we do not regard each obstacle we overcome as a destination in itself but rather part of the company's journey. We know, with the strong foundations we are building, the company can withstand whatever shock comes its way. Thinking back, I can say with great pride that throughout our sixty years we survived several crises, including two Gulf wars, the oil issues in the 1970s, the recession of the 1990s, and the 2008 global meltdown.

We are constantly working to ensure the company withstands all of its tests. We are constantly making sure all the gears are working and in place. We know that to continue on the path we have been on, one of success and growth, we cannot close our eyes for a moment or take any achievement for granted for even a split second. We constantly have to work for our success. Even our presence, as managers, has an impact. We are often the first ones in and the last ones out. It is an obligation we have to our people. Employees are inspired when they see us in the office or on the factory floor.

As the company management transitioned to his children, our father had more free time available, and this was when his charitable works began.

On leaving, he announced, "Since all of you got married, it's time for me to leave the business." My brother Simon recalls well that our father never *really* left the company. He might have retired in 1997, but he remained a vital consultant. I always tell people, "His work was his life, and his life was work."

Emil and Simon's undying dedication to hard work and professionalism is how the company remained successful after the handover.

I myself joined the company in 2001.

Antoine was able to witness, toward the end of his life, the commitment that his children had to the company. I think it was important that he saw his children following in his footsteps and that each child made the right decision to remain with the company.

"Sleep on a rock if you have to, since you are young."
—Antoine Nehme

I believe another right decision we made was to implement equal treatment for staff, something that was unusual for that part of the world. For the first time in a Middle Eastern company, women were on an equal footing with men. The idea of universal suffrage might be a mere 220 years old in Europe and the United States, but the Middle East is a different place. For women to have equal footing with that of men was revolutionary. It is still not something widely seen in traditional Middle Eastern institutions, but in the words of Bob Dylan, "The times they are changing."

From left to right: Rania, Emil, Antoine, Sheikh Hamad Bin Khalifah Al Thani,
Simon, and Alexander during a private audience with the Emir of the State of Qatar.

For my father, these concepts came naturally. We were all equals. He did not differentiate between daughter and son, which kept things harmonious. It helped to create a solid basis for decisions. It was similar to our company's policy of saying no to nepotism. We are all equal, and at the same time, we are all employed based on our skills and not our last names.

"It takes both sides to build a bridge."
—*Fredrik Nael*

This is important because we now always say to the extended family, "If you want to work in this company, you have to be qualified." When I was younger, travelling to recruit for the company and asking applicants about their qualifications, I used to wonder why nobody asked what qualified me to work at the company. I do not doubt that back then other candidates might have been better qualified than I was. I grew into my positions, learning through experience. Now, however, with the new generation, we want our extended family to have the necessary skills already in place.

We want to continue this process of ensuring we do not simply hire based on a last name or because someone in the family has a son or daughter who needs a job. Our rule that family must first work in another company and gain at least one promotion before applying to Nehmeh is what is fair to them, to the company, to our current employees, and to our customers who put so much faith in this company and its leadership. We took our father's policy of giving us an international education before bringing us into the family business a notch higher. We demanded that members of the family get experience outside the company before joining it. This policy tightens the nuts and bolts of the Nehmeh group, ensuring its longevity and growth to its fullest potential.

*"It takes a deep commitment to change
and an even deeper commitment to grow."*
—Ralph Ellison

Our own children, who are beginning to come of age and who may or may not enter the company, and our children's children, might devise different rules. We leave that up to them. I look forward to a time when there is minimal or zero involvement of the family in this organization. We know that the company will continue to be alive and well. It has succeeded in achieving its vision and has a new vision with even greater hopes and dreams.

Beyond the role of the family, the strength of the company has to do with the empowerment of our employees. Our company is based on people. If you do not give power to people to make decisions, to make mistakes, and to be able to call the shots and work with the relevant authorities, your company cannot grow. We have learned we need empowered employees for the future of our business. Empowerment, however, comes with the word *trust*, one of the values of Nehmeh. You cannot buy trust. Trust must be earned.

*"Learn from the mistakes of others.
You can never live long enough to make them all yourself."*
—Groucho Marx

We do like to think of ourselves as a model for businesses that care about their employees. It is not an easy ride. There are many things I struggle with personally every day. Among the things I struggle with most are the company's evolution and our process of modernizing it. There are many obstacles that we need to overcome, and the process is a constant battle, but I maintain positivity and remain hopeful about what the future will bring for our company.

Even with all the challenges, there is a strong sense of gratification about what we are doing and how we are accomplishing it.

With so many changes taking place, we ask ourselves at times, "Is this going to work?" Failure is a possibility with every new process. Still, for a solid company with sixty years of history and experience, failures will not mean disaster. We factor in the impact of failure when we test certain processes, knowing such failures would not be large enough to take the whole company down. Thus, we empower our employees to make decisions, knowing that not all of them will be correct at first. There is a learning curve for employees and for company leaders. This possibility of failure with new processes is a component of building experience and contributes to our knowledge base.

Governance

We are also in the process of changing the way we handle the company's governance, which involves how decisions are made and communicated and how they cascade down to absolutely every person in the organization. For example, we include our standard operating procedures (SOP) in our employee instruction manuals relevant to that person's department. We tell new staff and new management, "This is how we do things."

I must admit I dislike inefficiency and ineffectiveness, and I blame both of these things on bureaucracy (a.k.a. red tape). I hate all meaningless talks and meetings. I remember this phrase I heard once: if you're bored, just call a meeting. You hold a long stick. You show the charts. At the end of the day, even with coffee and donuts, what is being accomplished at most meetings? We never wish to become an ineffective dinosaur of an organization.

You cannot be sustainable with bureaucracy. Bureaucracy only builds more bureaucracy. On the other hand, there is an essential part for any company and that is the system and process of checks and balances. You need to have not only audits but also a well-thought-out system. This also means every business model is somewhat different. There is a top line and a bottom line, and something has to be produced and verified in between the two.

As leaders of the company and members of the founding family, we believe we must take all our employees by the hand and lead them across the bridge of the changes we are implementing. We continuously automate our processes. Yes, we do rely on technology, but we also rely on simplicity. We try to break down the processes and logistics into procedures that are easy for everyone to understand.

We know changes can be daunting and can also breed insecurity in our staff. People panic, worrying automation might mean the loss of jobs. However, that is far from the case. The end goal is to give our staff processes by which their career will not stall so they can move up in the company. When we explain that to people, there is a buy-in. This is where we win their hearts.

Not only are we looking to make our employees' lives simple, but we are also looking after their career at Nehmeh. For instance, we ask them, "Since you joined this company, has your career advanced? Have you followed your planned career path?" Sometimes, I get the reply, "No, I've stayed a clerk here."

My question then is, "Is this really what you want to do?" I always start with the same subject, "What's your dream? Where do you want to be in five years? Will you own a farm? Will you immigrate to Australia? Will you marry (or remarry)? Will you travel to the moon? What is your dream?" The dream could be anything and does not cost a penny.

People share and I reply, "This company has a dream too and a vision. Do you want to be a part of this vision?" I often use comic strips as an illustration of how life might be on the way to 2020.

One point I also make is that employees can also dream of leaving us. Many people in the past feared disclosing that they wanted to open their own business. They thought it would be frowned upon and would result in their losing their job.

The fact is that entrepreneurs beget entrepreneurs.

We actually welcome entrepreneurs. People are shocked when I tell them that my company is the correct place to learn business skills, even if employees learn them and then leave. We Nehme's were born to be entrepreneurs, and we continue our entrepreneurial journey. Where better for our employees to learn the challenges of opening a new business than with their current employer? They are instantly happy when they understand that their bosses understand them, even on a topic that other companies may find taboo.

Our vision contains heavy words such as innovation, sustainability, continuity, key players, and so on. We know these concepts may be hard to grasp in one go.

A form of an internal company-wide campaign.

We also use the concept of the high five. Just like the hands-in-the-air celebration athletes engage in after winning a goal, it is a way for us to celebrate successes and, at the same time, challenge each other to do better. The high five refers to our company's five years with five solutions, growing five times, and being in five different countries. Today all company employees, down to labourers and the most frazzled office workers, will understand the high five. This is one of the reasons for creating this graphic.

This graphic serves as an employee guide to our planned technology and initiatives. We liken it to Qatar's continual improvements. For instance, the country is installing a new mass-transit system, a subway system. With new tools for getting to work, our staff will be happy, and we feel it is the same way with new tools on the job. We want people to like it so much they whistle while they work.

In such an environment, employees will be empowered to make the right decisions. For example, we have technology allowing video conference calls with all our different branches. This technology was once science fiction like the *Dick Tracy* or *Star Trek* idea of talking to a watch and making a video call. The future is now. If technology allows employees to finish early, they can use that same technology to call the family, for example, and say, "Dear family, I'm coming home early. Wow! I work for a great company."

A happy employee can have a positive influence on others who doubt it is possible to love a job. His kid may say, "Papa, I want to work at your company." And the kid's mother says, "Yes, you will."

We dream, and we want our employees to share our dream.

Conclusion

I often say this to myself: "The success of a man is as visible in life as it is in death."

We want to ensure the values of Nehmeh are passed along to the future. As a timeless message.

We have survived several crises, and we have a legacy that we treat with sustainability. We are in the stages of, once again, passing the torch to new management. We move forward, ensuring the journey of Nehmeh continues no matter who is involved. This is what we value, and we know those who work with us, whether our employees or our clients—whom we cherish and who have helped us along this journey—cherish this too.

Any great movement, anything of substance on this planet always came about through the efforts of one person. One person decided he or she could no longer take the status quo and wanted to try something new or wanted to do something in a different way. As long as people have a message others can relate to, these movements will continue well into the future.

For those of us at Nehmeh, that person was our Antoine Nehme.

I follow his philosophy, and I use it to help my own employees in their day-to-day work with the company. Many employees tell me, "I'm struggling, but I feel I'm about to overcome my hurdles."

As long as we recognize there are great individuals who have done the world good and have given back to the community as a whole, we can maintain this high, incredible level of continuity into the future. For those of us leading Nehmeh, it is about the wow factor, something we expect from our employees and we give to our clients. This is the message we want to send out into the world.

While we excel at what we do, we remain modest. We Nehme's and those who work for us are, at heart, very humble people—a quality instilled in us from the very beginning.

He would say to us—and I have heard others say this too—"Keep your dreams in the clouds but your feet on the ground." Dream big. Dream humongous. There is no price tag for dreaming. Most importantly, dream big but ensure you do not miss out on opportunities that arise every day. You must ensure that when the knock of opportunity comes, you are not too lazy to answer.

"It matters not what someone is born, but what they grow to be."
—*J. K. Rowling*

Another saying that still resonates with me is that if there is no door, build one. What this means is that we must find a way for opportunity to happen. And this is what Antoine did—he acted upon opportunity time and time again. It is true that not all of us are born with the same chances when we start out. Some people may be born to more health, others to more wealth and connections; others though may not be as fortunate from birth. Sometimes, these hurdles are physical, such as being born with a disability. People must be willing to never stop learning for themselves and others.

"The purpose of learning is growth, and our minds, unlike our bodies, can continue growing as long as we live."
—Mortimer Adler

My father was in a continuous process of learning. I have saved the first e-mail he ever sent me because he wanted to learn e-mail, and I remember it as a special moment. Antoine came from the time of the telex and the telegram when every character had a price. He used to write "best regards" as "bst rgds" to save a few pennies for his children's schooling.

It is hard in this age of plenty to grasp the sacrifices this man made so that I can be here now, writing this book. With such blessings, I always tell people, you cannot really have a future if you do not know your past.

We live in an era when people do not care as much. At times, a lack of empathy is even considered acceptable, as exemplified by the horrible incidents involving young people on social media. For me, such an attitude could not be more wrong. And this lack of empathy also spills into politics. Many politicians will do things that they should not. This is a global issue. It is unfortunate that people do not learn from history and are accordingly deemed to repeat it.

"Nowadays people know the price of everything and the value of nothing."
—Oscar Wilde

My belief is that we must consult past experience: What did they do then? How did they do it? Hopefully, this book will somehow impart these ideas to you as you have read, and you will understand my father's legacy and his worldview.

This book therefore serves as an opportunity, one knocking on your door. We never know when such opportunities will knock again. Make sure to always preserve it. It gives you the model of a business born out of intense hardship, yet blossoming and thriving in a desert emirate. Your metaphoric desert may be anywhere—on ice or in an urban landscape. It does not matter. The same principles and ideas can apply to you whether you open a shop on the other side of the earth or invest close to home. It really does not matter as long as you have strong foundations.

Foundations give us strength. If you are constructing a building, the most important aspect is the foundation. You may build ten stories, but should an earthquake come, they could all topple down unless you have strong foundations. With strong foundation, nothing will destroy your construction or cause it harm—no flood, no earthquake.

This philosophy is relevant to people, relationships, and companies. As long as you have a strong foundation with your people, explaining who you are and how you do things, you will be successful. It is in this way that Nehmeh has been around for over six decades.

This is the transparency we live by. As long as our people and our clients know our company's history, they know the apple does not fall far from the tree. We are our father's children. This book, hopefully, reflects these values—The Nehmeh Way, the code of ethics we follow. This book may also serve as a foundation for you as well.

"No watchman on my work if my conscience is my watchman."
—*Antoine Nehme*

May your passing be a way long off, but after our deaths at some point in the next thirty or forty years, this book will remain. These writings will be the memory of how the company was founded by my father, Antoine Nehme. That great man will be remembered. Would I wish for his children to be remembered? That would be nice, but I am sure we will be remembered for the things we do for the next generation. We want to be a part of a success story that is timeless, boundless, real, and tangible.

As the children of Antoine Nehme, should we create other ventures in the future? Definitely. The sky is the limit for us, considering the foundation we have. Challenges will remain, but as a company and as a family, we will remain resilient, as we acknowledge that the glory is ahead of us and not just in the past. There are many people who live in the past, but we do not do so.

One must live in the present and think of what is to come. Passing the torch is a classic example, along with the family's transformation. Yet it all goes beyond this. It is also the story of longevity and dogged determination in the face of adversity. We believe it is nice to be a company that cares not just about reputation but also resources, from people to materials to its valued clients.

We look at our history and remember we do not want to idolize or create monuments for the man who founded our company. Instead, our goal is to give him the respect he deserves. Antoine Nehme received enormous respect in his lifetime. I think we owe him respect in his death, something to give to a new generation of employees and family.

Antoine Nehme on his eightieth birthday in 2010.

Eulogy of our dearly departed

> The passing is usually a moment of sadness and grief, but we look to it as a memory of happy times instead, and that includes his smiling picture, which we wish to remember him by.
>
> He was a big man, in all meanings of the word: his height, his voice, and his character and no doubt, his presence was prominent.
>
> He welcomed us, as boys and a girl, but leaves us as men and a woman.
>
> His memory will live on for all time.
>
> *—as read by Antoine Nehme's eldest son, Emil*

Alfred, my father's brother, said it best: "There is no denying Antoine is the one who elevated the standards of all the Nehme families."

Rania, my father's daughter, said it in her own way: "For the happiness that you show, for the lightness, for the light, for the return of the smile, for the eyes wide open, for the wonder in those eyes, for the anticipation, for the eagerness to learn, and for the unconditional love."

I remember reading somewhere that to value someone's life, we must look at three dimensions: breadth (how many people that person touched), depth (how deeply that person was touched), and consistency (how frequently that person touched). Full marks go to Antoine Nehme.

> *"I want to be all used up when I die."*
> —*George Bernard Shaw*

Thus, we move forward. This is what Antoine Nehme would have surely wished for. Personally, I would like to be able to look back ten years from today and say we - as caretakers of this generation - were successful in doing our part in continuing the story of Nehmeh into the future. Although our heritage and values are timeless, Nehmeh will inevitably continue to reinvent itself one way or another (whether in the industries it serves, the territories it covers or even its shareholder-base) all as part of its evolution. By sparing no efforts in the name of betterment, the conscience can remain at peace whether at the present or in the times to come.

> *"The most beautiful people we have known are those who have known defeat, known suffering, known struggle, known loss, and have found their way out of the depths. These persons have an appreciation, a sensitivity, and an understanding of life that fills them with compassion, gentleness, and a deep loving concern. Beautiful people do not just happen."*
> —*Elisabeth Kübler-Ross*

May you too find & identify your own *blessings in the sand*, in whatever shape your *blessings* manifest themselves into and wherever your *sand* may be.

Thank you for being part of the journey into the life and legacy of a man known as Antoine Nehme who chose to do the extra with the ordinary.

Index

Printed in the USA
CPSIA information can be obtained
at www.ICGtesting.com
JSHW072029140824
68134JS00045B/3842

9 781599 326863